An Ocean
of Words

An Ocean *of* Words

A Dictionary of Nautical Words and Phrases

Peter D. Jeans

Illustrated by
Ross H. Shardlow

A Birch Lane Press Book • Published by Carol Publishing Group

For Judith, Romony, and Simon

First Carol Publishing Group edition published 1998.
Copyright © 1993 Peter D. Jeans

A Birch Lane Press Book
Published by Carol Publishing Group

Birch Lane Press is a registered trademark of Carol Communications, Inc.
Editorial, sales and distribution, and rights and permissions inquires should be addressed to Carol Publishing Group, 120 Enterprise Avenue, Secaucus, N.J. 07094
In Canada: Canadian Manda Group, One Atlantic Avenue, Suite 105, Toronto, Ontario M6K 3E7

Carol Publishing books may be purchased in bulk at special discounts for sales promotion, fundraising, or educational purposes. Special editions can be created to specifications. For details, contact Special Sales Department, 120 Enterprise Avenue, Secaucus, N.J. 07094

Manufactured in the United States of America

10 9 8 7 6 5 4 3 2 1

This Birch Lane Press book, first printed in 1998, was originally published under the title *Ship to Shore,* in 1993. This edition, reprinted by permission of ABC-CLIO, is a retitled, abridged version.

Library of Congress Cataloging-in-Publication Data

Jeans, Peter D.
　　An ocean of words : a dictionary of nautical words and phrases / Peter D. Jeans ;
illustrated by Ross H. Shardlow. — 1st Carol Pub. Group ed.

　　　　p.　　cm.
　　Abridged version of : Ship to shore. 1993.
　　ISBN 1–55972–450–1 (hc)
　　1. English language—Etymology—Dictionaries. 2. Sailors— Language—Dictionaries. 3. Naval art and science—Dictionaries. 4. English language—Terms and phrases. 5. Seafaring life— Dictionaries. 6. Figures of speech. I. Jeans, Peter D. Ship to shore II. Title.
　　PE1583.J42　　1998
　　422'.03—dc21　　　　　　　　　　　　　　　　97-44144
　　　　　　　　　　　　　　　　　　　　　　　　　　CIP

Contents

No man will be a sailor who has contrivance enough to get himself into a jail; for being in a ship is being in a jail, with the chance of being drowned.

DR. SAMUEL JOHNSON

Acknowledgments

I would like to record my deep appreciation to my family for their encouragement and forbearance during the four years that I worked on this book. It takes a certain kind of understanding to be able to live with a person whose passion of the moment demands that the family home be endlessly littered with dictionaries, histories, novels, and the like—anything and everything, as long as it has to do with the sea.

For rather similar reasons I thank my colleagues of the '80s in the English Department at Willetton Senior High School, Perth, Western Australia, each of whom maintained a stoic patience far beyond the demands of duty and loyalty when their every utterance was subjected to an immediate litmus test for nautical parentage.

I warmly thank my original typist, Mrs. Pat Bishop, whose personal interest and professional concern with the original draft made my task of editing so much easier. My daughter Romony has earned my everlasting gratitude for her cheerfulness and skill in keyboarding the whole of the large typescript into the family computer. The title of this book is the result of a brilliant flash of serendipity on the part of my wife Judith.

Various friends have read through parts of the manuscript for me and have made a number of valuable suggestions as to how it might be improved. I am indebted to the following people for their interest and specific ideas: Donald Burnside, Rob and Denise Main, Brendan Mulvey, David Price, and Judy Semple. Terry Woodings went to painstaking lengths in tracking down information about conditions of life in the sailing navy of Olde England, and I thank him here most warmly for his enthusiastic help.

The illustrations that greatly enhance this book were done by Ross Shardlow. Ross has given me many hours of his time in enlightening me on some of the finer points of ship design and construction; he has also suggested the inclusion of a dozen or more of the main dictionary entries, and I will always remain grateful for his friendship and for the fact that he so readily shared his extraordinary maritime knowledge with me.

Finally, I gladly acknowledge the encouragement given to me very early in the project by my friend Dr. Andrew Ong, whose enthusiasm for hard work helped to keep me going at my own task.

Peter D. Jeans
Perth, Western Australia

Introduction

My aim in this work is to illustrate what I believe is the astonishing debt that our idiomatic speech owes to the nautical language of the past. English is extraordinarily rich in metaphor, and it is the intention of this book to show that many of the figures of speech that we use from day to day derive from the language and customs of the sea.

I have also included a relatively small number of nautical terms that in themselves are not part of our daily idiomatic coinage, yet because of their prevalence and importance in the literature of the sea are reasonably familiar to the general reader as belonging to matters maritime, such as "Davy Jones's Locker."

This project began through an almost accidental meeting with the nautical origin of the expression "Between the devil and the deep blue sea," which refers clearly enough to the situation where a person is faced with a choice between two risky or undesirable courses of action. What with being menaced by the devil on the one hand and the perils of the sea on the other, the phrase seemed perfectly self explanatory; but when I happened to come across an account of a ship's crew engaged in recaulking the seams of their leaky vessel, with great emphasis being laid on the difficulty of paying and pitching the two seams known as the devil seams, I was intrigued: perhaps the devil in the metaphor was not Old Nick himself, as I had otherwise always believed.

And indeed, this proved to be the case, as the reader will discover in the two entries under *Devil:* "Between the devil and the deep blue sea," and "The devil to pay."

Putting aside the expressions that were quite obviously nautical in origin, I then began to pay particular attention to the language used by such writers as Richard Henry Dana (*Two Years Before the Mast*), Frank Bullen (*The Cruise of the Cachalot),* and the contemporary novelist Patrick O'Brian (the "Jack Aubrey" series), to name but a few. In them I discovered that such ordinary, everyday expressions as "to rummage," "to flog a dead horse," "to break new ground," and others discussed in this dictionary were in fact born at sea as part of the jargon that English-speaking seamen have used for many hundreds of years.

How many other words and phrases that we use in our own daily life, I wondered, are in fact coinages from the very different world of the professional seaman? With this in mind I began a search, first through the literature that deals exclusively with nautical expressions (such as Rogers and Lind), and later through those books that treat the seafaring life in all its many aspects (such as Falconer, Harland, Hakluyt, and Kemp).

Armed with a very lengthy list, I then checked each term that was not obviously nautical against the best general and etymological dictionaries to which I had access. A decision to admit any particular term into this present work (or, of course, to exclude it) depended on a combination of what these reference works had to say and what I had learned over a lifetime of teaching English and, in particular, reading very widely in the nautical field.

Some of the most useful texts that I consulted were *The Country Life Book of Nautical Terms under Sail* by Whitlock and others; Falconer's *Universal Dictionary of the Marine,* Smyth's *The Sailor's Word Book,* Dana's *Two Years Before the Mast,* Hakluyt's *Voyages and Documents,* Harland's *Seamanship in the Age of Sail,* Kemp's *The Oxford Companion to Ships and the Sea,* Masefield's *Sea Life in Nelson's Time,* and Morton's *The Wind Commands.*

There are several books available that deal with nautical terms as they are used in our daily speech, but with the exception of Rogers they tend to be shallow in range, superficial in treatment, and rarely do they treat the language background of their subject. This is where, I believe, this present work has something to offer; it is a serious attempt to document a portion of the linguistic heritage that has been passed down to us by whole generations of seafarers, and it offers a clear indication of where the word came from, hence the inclusion of etymologies for most of the terms in this dictionary.

I have tried to position this work for a readership that has an interest in language not necessarily as linguists or language specialists, but as reasonably informed readers who sometimes wonder about the words and expressions that they use in their daily speech. I have also endeavoured to write for those readers who have an interest in the sea, perhaps the professional seafarer, or the sometime voyager, or that much-maligned species, the armchair sailor.

Language has always been of concern and interest to people; it is my hope that this dictionary will encourage an even greater interest in what I consider to be a rich and fascinating topic: the idiom and metaphor that, over the centuries, has been passed on from ship to shore.

An Ocean
of Words

A1
To be in A1 condition

A1 is the old and famous classification given by *Lloyd's Register of Shipping* to vessels as an indication of their state of seaworthiness. The letter refers to hulls that meet Lloyd's requirements concerning materials and method of construction. The numeral refers to a vessel's ground tackle; if her anchors, cables, and such meet Lloyd's standards, then they are given the classification *1*. Thus, to be "A1" was to be first rate, the very best. The more modern system uses the notation *100 A1,* but the older classification is still widely used and has since the eighteenth century gone into colloquial usage to designate anything that is of the best quality.

A.B.

The abbreviation for the term *able-bodied;* it is not the initials of the two words, as is often thought, but originally was simply the first two letters of *able.* To be rated able-bodied in the old sailing days, a man had to be able to hand, reef, and steer; that is, he had to be skilled in all the facets of handling sails, and had to be able to steer with skill in any weather. In the modern navy, of course, a seaman must have many more skills than that. There were three rates of seaman: A.B., Ordinary Seaman, Landsman. The term came to be used ashore to refer to anyone who was healthy and strong, fit enough to carry out the task intended for him or her.

4

Aback
To be taken aback

The sails of a square-rigger were said to be "aback" when the wind was blowing directly on the wrong or foremost side of the sails. In certain ship-handling manoeuvres, putting the sails aback was deliberate; at other times, it could create a dangerous situation, because a sudden shift in the wind, especially a gale-force wind, could cause considerable damage to spars and rigging if the officers and crew weren't alert to the threat.

Colloquially, the term means to be surprised or to be confronted with an unexpected situation or development, as a consequence of which one is at a loss as to what to do or say next.

Account
To be on the account

An old phrase meaning to sail off on a piratical expedition; the term was often used by buccaneers to describe their rather irregular way of life at sea. The phrase is intended to sound a little more polite than "turning pirate," and probably derived from the fact that a would-be pirate so arranged his affairs that he would be able to account for his actions if caught and charged with illegal practices. More loosely, *to be on the account* means to be ready to benefit from any situation that arises.

Addle

The seaman's name for water that had gone stale or putrid in the cask. This occurred so frequently that many ships carried large quantities of beer, which kept much longer than did fresh water. The expression came to mean muddled or confused, spoiled or rotten. From the Old English *adela,* liquid filth. Colloquially, anything that is addled is muddled or confused.

Ahead

In front of the ship, in the direction toward which her bow is pointing. From the Old English prefix *on,* meaning on, in, into, to, toward; and the Old English *heafod,* head (of the body).

To go ahead

". . . it was necessary that a man should go ahead with a sword to cut away the creepers."

—Charles Darwin (1809–1882), English naturalist, *Voyage Round the World* (1870)

Originally a purely nautical word, and one of many that has the preposition *a* as prefix so as to indicate, precisely and economically, direction and amount—a consideration of particular importance to sailors who are required quickly and efficiently to handle a vessel under all conditions of sea and battle. Other examples of such peremptory orders are "abaft," "abreast," "ahoy," "a-lee," "avast," "astern," and "aloof."

Ahead, of course, means in front of the ship, in the direction toward which she is pointing. To go ahead means just that: to move forward. As an expression it means to proceed (often with permission implied), to take the lead, to be in the forefront.

Ahoy!

The standard hailing cry of the sailor to attract attention. From the interjection *a* + *hoy*, a small coasting vessel, sometimes called a sloop or a smack. A coasting vessel is one that keeps the coast in sight when sailing from one port to another; such vessels use coastal landmarks by which to navigate, rather than stellar navigation. Often used in everyday idiomatic speech, as in "Ahoy there! What do you think you're doing with that spade?"

When a small naval craft approaches another naval ship at its mooring, the gangway sentry challenges the smaller vessel with the standard cry "Boat ahoy!" The coxswain of the visiting boat replies in one of a number of ways: if his boat is carrying any member of the royal family, he would cry "Standard!," a reference to the royal standard that his boat would be wearing (by day, of course, such a challenge would be unnecessary, as the gangway sentry would see, and would certainly know beforehand of, the royal personage's approach).

Should the boat have a member of the Admiralty aboard, the coxswain would reply "Admiralty!" With an admiral or commander-in-chief aboard, the coxswain answers the challenge with "Flag!" followed by the name of the flag officer's ship. With a captain on board the visiting small craft, the reply is merely the name of the ship that the captain commands. If the passengers are officers other than the captain, the coxswain replies "Aye, aye!" and if there are no officers at all the reply is "No, no!" Strictly speaking, even the Archbishop of Canterbury as a passenger would merit only a "No, no!" from the coxswain, but in fact the coxswain would reply "Aye, aye!" to ensure that the distinguished visitor was received aboard the warship with proper courtesy.

Aloof
To keep aloof

"Thy smile and frown are not aloof / From one another."

—Alfred, Lord Tennyson (1809–1892), English poet, *Madeline*

To keep the ship's head as close as possible to the wind, to keep away to windward; from the Middle English *lof.* Now rendered as "luff," "to luff up," "to keep your luff." From this nautical usage is derived the modern meaning of *aloof*: to keep at a distance from, to stand apart from, to keep away from.

Ardent

"Ardent and intrepid on the field of battle, Monmouth was everywhere else effeminate and irresolute."

—Thomas Babington Macaulay (1800–1859), British historian and politician, *History of England* (1848)

A very old term from seafaring days; it referred to a ship's propensity for rounding up to (i.e., turning into) the wind unless firm control was kept on the tiller or wheel. Light weather helm is a desirable characteristic in sailing vessels, because if the helmsman falls overboard the craft will repeatedly round up into the wind, thus losing way and giving him at least a chance of climbing back on board.

The word found its way into English metaphor to mean earnest, passionate, and fervent, from the apparent desire of a ship to seek the wind. It comes from the Latin *ardere,* to burn.

B

Back
To put one's back into it

To do something with all one's energy and strength; to give the task all of one's effort. A phrase in wide use at sea, especially in encouraging a pulling boat's crew to work hard. From the fact that pulling on an oar requires, among other things, a strong back.

Backwash

Originally, the water thrown back by the motor, oars, or paddle wheels of a small boat or other vessel. Now also a figure of speech meaning a condition that lasts after the event that caused it, as in an argument, debate, political matters, and the like.

Backwater

"Mr Temple, on reaching the backwater of a river which had been quite shallow in the morning, found it ten feet deep."

—*The Reader*,
vol. 2, no. 47, November 21, 1863

A body of water unaffected by tidal or other forces, usually stagnant, always quiet and peaceful; hence the figurative application to a small town or village that is off the beaten track, a place not affected by what is happening in the world outside, usually because of its isolation.

Bale
To bale out

A bale (often spelled "bail") is a bucket or other vessel used for baling or scooping water out of a yacht or ship's boat, when the pumps are not working. Commonly used as an order to make a parachute jump from an aeroplane; it also means to abandon a dangerous position or course of action, as a member of a diving group might decide to withdraw from a proposed expedition to a wreck on a dangerous reef. The ground-sense is from the idea of emptying or evacuation, as in the original usage. From the French *baille,* bucket, and deriving from the Latin *aquae baiula,* water-bearer.

Balk

"The thorny ground is sure to balk / All hopes of harvest there."

—William Cowper (1731–1800), English writer, *Olney Hymns: The Sower* (1779)

An old term for naval timber imported from the Baltic countries as large, squared beams. From the Anglo-Saxon *balca,* ridge, and the Old Norse *balkr,* hedge, boundary. *To balk* is to put an obstacle or stumbling block in someone's path, to check another's freedom, in the same way that a timber (a beam, a frame, or some such) can be a hindrance or act as a boundary to one's sphere of movement. Found, for example, as the "balk line" in the game of billiards.

Bamboozle

A slang word that many people believe to be American in origin, but in fact it seems to have begun life as a cant word in England, probably in the purlieus of London in the late seventeenth century (it is attested in print as early as 1703), and is among what Jonathan Swift called, in the *Tatler* (no. 230; November 1710), "certain words invented by some pretty fellows, such as Banter, Bamboozle." *(Pretty fellows* is itself a term from that period, meaning flash folk, thieves, robbers, and the like.) *Bamboozle* meant then, as it does now, to cheat, to swindle, to deceive.

"Let no one be bamboozled by this kind of talk."

—Edward A. Freeman, *Times of London,* February 10, 1877

What is certain is that the word *bamboozle* was used by British seamen to describe the Spanish practice of hoisting false colours (flags) to deceive the enemy. Any note of indignation from the British of that period should be ignored, as they were just as assiduous as every other maritime nation in following this hallowed custom of the sea.

Bandanna

Also "bandana." A cotton neckerchief or scarf, usually brightly coloured (white designs on a bright red or blue background being the most popular), worn by seamen in the nineteenth century as a head covering, head band, or neck cloth; sometimes also as a waist band. A Hindi word, introduced into English by British seamen and the military. From the Hindustani *bandhnu,* a mode of dyeing in which the cloth is tied in such a way as to prevent parts of it from receiving the dye.

Bang-up time

Seamen's slang for celebration of a special occasion; probably from the fact that a successful hit with the ship's guns was cause for much loud cheering among the crew. Now a metaphor to mean first-rate.

Barbecue

"Oldfield, with more than harpy throat endued, Cries, Send me, gods, a whole hog barbecued."

—Alexander Pope (1688–1744), cited in the *Universal Dictionary of the*

This is the well-known method of cooking food outdoors, popular particularly in Australia, America, and New Zealand; in all these countries the word can refer to the informal social event that usually accompanies this kind of outdoor cooking (also called a "cookout" in America). Essentially, a barbecue is a metal frame or grill for cooking meat above an open fire of coals, wood, or the like.

The word is from the Spanish *barboka.* The connection with maritime usage is that, in the early days of piracy in the Pacific and the Caribbean, these privateers became known as "buccaneers" from the French *boucan,* grill, or the cooking of dried meat over an open fire. Buccaneers (later known as "pirates") became closely involved with the illegal trading in such meat throughout the Caribbean. Thus, the innocent and enjoyable pastime of having a barbecue in one's own backyard owes its origin to the bloody history of piracy on the Spanish Main.

Barrel
Over a barrel

Sometimes expressed as "over the barrel." To be in a predicament, a jam, from which there is no apparent way out. The term originates from the days when a seaman under punishment was spread-eagled over a gun barrel for a flogging (also known as "to marry the gunner's daughter"). To have someone over a barrel is to be in a position to get whatever one wants from that person.

Beachcomber

"Here was a change in my life as complete as it had been sudden. In the twinkling of an eye I was transformed from a sailor into a 'beach-comber' and a hide-curer . . ."

—Richard Henry Dana (1815–1882), *Two Years Before the Mast* (1840)

Originally a word to describe waves that habitually crash onto the shore, such as the long-crested waves to be found in many parts of the Pacific, particularly around the islands of Hawaii; the action of the wave was likened to that of a comb as it thundered onto the sand and withdrew again into the sea (a comber is any long curling wave; *beachcomber* described those waves that reached the shore). The word became a metaphor for seamen who preferred to hang around ports and harbours, living on the charity of others rather than work; such a person often wandered up and down the beaches looking for flotsam and jetsam that might prove saleable.

The term now more generally describes any loafer around the waterfront, particularly in the "lotus" islands of the Pacific; many followers of the surfing craze were also called beachcombers because they seemed to do no useful work. The word in this form is said to have originated in New Zealand in about 1844.

Beach is from the Anglo-Saxon *bece,* brook. The word for what we call the beach today was the Anglo-Saxon *strand,* found in cognate forms in the other Teutonic languages, for example, the Dutch *strand,* and Icelandic *strand. Bece* then became *-beach* in many English place names, such as Wisbech and Holbeach, and gradually the meaning was transferred from pebbly brook to the pebbly shore (one needs to remember that many of the beaches of England are composed of pebbles or shingle).

"The waves combed over the vessel."

—William Clark Russell (1844–1911), cited in *Shorter Oxford English Dictionary* (1962)

Comb is from the Anglo-Saxon *camb,* German *kamm,* Old Norse *kambr,* a common Teutonic word that derives ultimately from the Sanskrit *quambas,* tooth. The application of *comber* to describe the typical Pacific wave drew attention to the notion of the breaking wave's lip seeming to be like a comb in action as the wave reared a foaming crest, was flung forward, and then crashed down into itself.

Beaker

Any cylindrical drinking vessel with a flat bottom, commonly made of plastic or glass and usually provided with a wide mouth, and (in laboratories) fitted with a pouring spout. The word comes from the Spanish *barrico,* a wooden cask filled with fresh water and kept permanently stored in a ship's boat as an emergency ration should the vessel be wrecked.

The seaman pronounced the word as "breaker," although it was always given the Spanish spelling *barrico,* having been used by seamen in this form since the sixteenth century. It possibly stems from the earlier Spanish *bareca,* a small wooden keg. The Anglicised form *beaker* is still in common use, the first *r* having disappeared because of the fancied resemblance of the pouring spout to a bird's beak.

Beam
To be on one's beam ends

"For many a busy hand toiled there, Strong pales to shape and beams to square."
—Sir Walter Scott (1771–1832), Scottish man of letters, *Lay of the Last Minstrel* (1805)

A vessel is on her beam ends when she has been laid completely on her side by very heavy weather, such that her deck beams are vertical or nearly so. The beams are the transverse timbers stretching across the vessel from side to side at right angles to the keel. To be on her beam ends is a particularly dangerous position for any vessel. The colloquialism is used to describe the situation in which a person finds himself when driven to his last shift, his final resources; when she is broke, down and out, and with little hope of succour.

Bear

From the Anglo-Saxon *beran* and the Sanskrit *bhar,* to hold or support, also to remain firm. All the intransitive senses (for example, "to bear with") are originally nautical.

To bear down upon

To approach from the weather side, from upwind, from the position of advantage (for sailing ships, the weather gage). Colloquially, the phrase suggests intimidation, as from a position of superior advantage; to bear down upon somebody is to bring all one's guns to bear upon that person, so to speak.

To bear in with

When a vessel sails so as to join or accompany another vessel, she is said "to bear in with" it; to come closer to, to sail in company. Also used when approaching land or a certain landmark: to bear in with the land, to sail closer to it so as to pick up identifying marks. The colloquialism is much the same: to bear in with someone, a crowd, etc., is to join with.

To bear up

"A religious hope does not only bear up the mind under her sufferings, but makes her rejoice in them."

—Joseph Addison (1672–1719), English poet and essayist, cited in the *Universal Dictionary of the English*

Colloquially, to keep one's spirits up, to not lose one's courage in the face of adversity. From the order to the helmsman to "bear up," to bring the vessel even closer to the wind. Such a course always means a much wetter and generally more difficult thrash to windward; hence the metaphor of gritting one's teeth for the duration.

Bell–bottomed trousers

Many readers will be familiar with the old music-hall song that began,

> "Bell-bottomed trousers, coats of navy blue,
> She loves a sailor and a sailor loves her too."

After the establishment of a standard uniform for sailors in 1857, it became possible for the men to buy their own lengths of blue serge (of the navy-pattern colour) so that they could have their own best shore-going clothes (their number one suits or "rigs") made up by the "jewing firm," the group of sailors who were authorised to do tailoring on board ship.

By using the whole width of the bolt of serge, and thereby avoiding waste, the Royal Navy seaman was able to introduce the full, bell-bottomed trouser that has long since been a mark of his naval uniform. The distinctive crease that the seaman gave to his bell-bottomed rig was achieved by a method of folding each leg inside to outside in concertina fashion, dampening them with water, and pressing them between stiff cardboards, large books, or other heavy objects.

Bender   The famous drinking spree that a person will embark upon to celebrate some noteworthy occasion; it usually involves an expedition that encompasses every public house within reach, with the sole object of getting as drunk as possible. Workers employed in hazardous jobs (such as putting out dangerous oil-well fires) might go on a bender to relieve the considerable stresses of the job.

The expression, which is nautical in origin, may reflect a seaman's pun: to get drunk is to be "tight," and a "bend" is a shipboard knot that is tight.

Berth   Probably from the seaman's use of *bear,* in the sense of direction. In its oldest sense, *berth* means convenient sea room, and all later meanings of the word have evolved from this original nautical usage. This is a good example of how our everyday language has willingly accepted nautical metaphor.

To give a wide berth   The place where a vessel is moored or anchored is called its "berth." *To give a wide berth* is to not come near a person, to keep at a safe distance from him or her; literally, it means to give a ship plenty of room in which to swing at anchor while lying at her moorings. This is the oldest meaning of the expression; all others derive from this usage.

Binge To binge means to rinse out, or "bull," a cask to prepare it for new contents. Casks were an essential part of a ship's equipment for they were the only means of carrying food and water over lengthy voyages; hence, great care was taken of them.

Binge is also a colloquialism for a spree, a period of excessive indulgence in drink especially, or food. Probably derived from the sailor's love of spirits, which he might occasionally have been able to steal when bingeing a cask. From the Lincolnshire dialect word binge, to soak.

Bitter
To the bitter end Relentlessly, unceasingly, as in "He saw it through to the bitter end," to the last stroke of adverse fortune. The phrase is from the sailor's name for the inboard end of rope or cable that is secured or belayed to the bitts to prevent it being lost overboard: this is literally the bitter end. The bitts were very strong timbers especially constructed for securing anchor

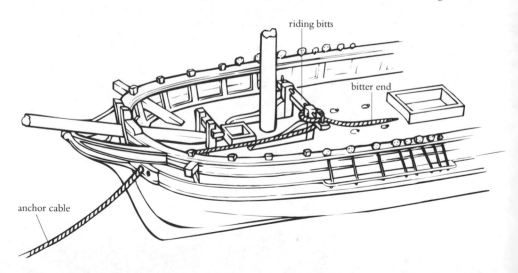

riding bitts

bitter end

anchor cable

cable inboard of the vessel; they were also used for securing
some of the rigging. When a vessel is riding to her anchor,
the part of her anchor cable that lies abaft the bitts is the
bitter end; to pay a rope or chain out to the bitter end
means that all of it has been paid out and no more remains
to be let go.

From the Old Norse *biti,* cross-beam. The expression is
not in any way connected to *bitter* in the sense of evil, sour,
or unpleasant.

Black list
To be on the black list

A list of those in disgrace, or those who have incurred
censure or punishment. Originally a list of sailors
undergoing punishment; probably deriving from the term
black books, which, because of their close association with
the laws, customs, and usages of the sea, came to be
associated with the awarding of punishment.

Blazer

The jacket or coat well known by school children, members
of teams, and others as an element of a uniform. Originally
it was an item of dress devised by Captain Washington of
HMS *Blazer* in 1845, who dressed his crew in special
blue-and-white striped jerseys or guernseys. Accordingly, the
crew became known as the "Blazers," from which is derived
the term used for the garment today.

Blood money

"It is not laufull to put them
into the God's chest,
for it is bloudmoney."

—Matthew 25:6,
Miles Coverdale Bible (1535)

Originally money paid to an agent, such as the keeper of an
inn or boardinghouse, for the procurement of men to fill
vacancies in a ship's crew. The expression has gained a
number of wider meanings in colloquial speech: a fee paid
to a hired murderer; compensation paid to the relative of a
slain man; and small remuneration earned by great effort, as
in the old days of sweated labour in factories. The expression
is also said to derive from the bounty paid by the British
Admiralty for the capture of smugglers and their boats in

the nineteenth century. The payment was 20 pounds for each smuggler captured and convicted.

Blowhard   Sailor's slang for a wind-bag, a talkative show-off who sets out to impress his audience with tales that reflect only credit on himself. In British and Australian slang, a "skite" (from the Scottish *blatherskate* and the Old Norse *blathra,* to talk stupidly). The allusion was to the windy words of self-praise, as if the speaker were all wind, hot air, without substance, in the way that the wind often blows endlessly at sea; also, the insubstantiality of the wind itself. An expression still common in Australia.

Blubber   To weep, to shed tears; an allusion to the way in which oil ran in small globules from whale blubber or fat. The language of the whalers is an important source of metaphor in our own daily speech, although it did not contribute as freely as did the merchant service and, particularly, the British navy during its supremacy of the global seas between the sixteenth and twentieth centuries.

Blue Ribbon   Also "Blue Riband." The ad hoc trophy awarded to the passenger vessel that made the fastest crossing of the Atlantic; the contest was unofficial but nevertheless various national lines competed earnestly for it because of the status gained by winning. The first vessel to hold the Blue Ribbon was a Cunard liner, the *Acadia,* built in 1840; the last was the *United States* in 1952, with a speed of nearly 36 knots.

So prestigious was this award that the blue ribbon became the emblem of supremacy in all sorts of contests. It is, for example, given as a kind of laurel to winning exhibits in agricultural shows, horse shows, and other contests. The main event in a competition is often called the "blue ribbon event."

The colour blue was almost certainly chosen because of its long association with royalty and nobility. The expression *blue blood* denotes high or noble birth; the notion originated in Spain from the fact that the veins of the pure-blooded Spanish aristocrat appeared to be more blue than those of other Spaniards of mixed ancestry, especially those with a Moorish connection.

Bone
To have a bone in her teeth

A "bone" is the foam formed at the bow or cutwater as the vessel moves through the water. When the foam is quite marked, the ship is said to have "a bone in her teeth." More loosely, it is applied to a person or conveyance of some kind that is moving along very freely and briskly, with an air of determination and purpose.

"bone"
(bow wave)

Boobs

Seaman's slang term for a woman's breasts; from *booby,* a large, robust seabird that was remarkable for its inability to take fright at the approach of a human. The seaman regarded a woman's breasts in much the same light as he regarded everything else in the world about him: Was it functional? Did it work? Clearly, insofar as his own needs were concerned, the female mammaries were a useless article; to this end they were "stupid," and so shared similar traits with the booby bird. The expression has firmly established itself in everyday speech.

Booby

"Then let the boobies stay at home."

—William Cowper (1731–1800), *The Yearly Distress,* cited in the *Universal Dictionary of the English Language* (1897).

The well-known tropical seabird. It prefers to rest out of water at night, often perching on the yards of ships. The name is from the Spanish *bob,* fool; the bird was considered stupid because it allowed itself to be so easily caught by seamen, it having no apparent sense of danger. The word is used aboard in *booby hatch,* a small hatchway with a sliding cover; and ashore in expressions such as "booby prize" and "booby trap." A booby (sometimes "boob") is a stupid person, a fool.

Booming
To boom along

To boom along or *to be booming along* is to sail, move, crack on at a great pace, "to have a bone in her teeth." A sailing ship under full sail and with studding sails set (additional fair-weather sails set out on special booms) was said to be "booming along." Colloquially, the phrase means to be moving along in some enterprise at a fast pace, without hindrance.

Bowing and scraping

"...bowing and scraping and rubbing his hands together."

—Anthony Trollope (1815–1882), English novelist, cited in the *Universal Dictionary of the English Language* (1897)

In the Royal Navy, an officer's cocked hat was nicknamed a "scraper"; hence the origin of the colloquial expression "bowing and scraping." *To bow and scrape* originally meant removing one's headgear in salute to a superior officer and then bowing to express even greater respect; it now means to be servile toward someone, to show humility.

Brass
As bold as brass

From the appearance of the highly polished brasswork on a ship, which of course served no real purpose in the working of the vessel; it was for show only. Colloquially, the expression means very bold, usually impertinent.

Brass tacks
To get down to brass tacks

To get down to the basics or fundamentals of a problem or situation; to deal with basic principles. Lind (see bibliography) states that linoleum was often used to cover the deck, and that brass tacks were employed to nail it down to the planking. This writer has never encountered any reference to linoleum being used at sea for this purpose, but it does not seem unreasonable—at least for cabins, the tween-decks, the flats, and such. It would be unthinkable to have "lino" as a surfacing on the main deck of any vessel. The expression may also owe something to Cockney rhyming slang, in which brass tacks are facts.

The expression would have appealed to seamen because brass did not corrode at sea as did iron, and also because sailors took considerable pride in keeping the ship's brightwork (brass fittings, varnished railings, and so on) in good condition.

Bucket
To kick the bucket

An old colloquialism, susceptible of at least three explanations, only one of them being nautical. *To kick the bucket* is to die, or to involve oneself in serious trouble.

According to one explanation, the beam from which pigs were suspended for slaughtering was called a "bucket," from the Old French *buquet* and the later French *trebucket,* a balance; the pig, in dying, literally kicked the bucket. Another version is that the would-be human suicide often used a bucket to stand on, which he then kicked away from under him the better to hang himself.

The third explanation rests on the well-known seafaring superstition that to lose, or accidentally kick, a bucket overboard was a serious mishap, not to be lightly dismissed. The reason for this is that, as a receptacle, a bucket is of great importance to the seaman: it is his bailer when his vessel is taking in water, and it is of great use for catching rainwater when shipboard supplies are low. It also has many other day-to-day uses in the routine of life at sea. It would seem that this last is the most likely explanation behind the expression if only because, as a body, seamen have over the centuries had the profoundest effect upon our language, an effect greater, I believe, than any other occupational class of people in the history of our tongue.

Bumpkin An awkward, clumsy sort of person (a "country bumpkin"); the archetypal country yokel. From the diminutive of the Dutch *boom,* tree, spar, and found in the nautical word *bumkin,* a short boom projecting outwards from the stern. The connection lies in the stolid "woodenness" of both the boom and the clumsy yokel.

By and by Also "bye and bye." To sail a vessel "by the wind" is to sail her as close to the wind as she will go, with all sheets hardened in and the bow pointing into the wind as much as possible. A seaman says that his vessel is sailing "by and by" when she is making very slow progress against the wind; the doubling of *by* in the phrase is an intensifier, to indicate the degree of difficulty encountered and the slowness of the ship's progress. *By and by* as a colloquialism means after a short time, soon, in the near future.

By and large Taking one thing with another; all things considered; generally speaking. From the fact that when a vessel is sailing into the wind (i.e., when she is close-hauled), if she sails a little off the wind—that is, frees her wind a point or so—she is said to be sailing "by and large." She is near the wind but not fully on it, so that the leading edge of each sail is still setting almost as close to the wind as it will go, but yet just sufficiently free that it maintains an efficient shape. The colloquialism derives its meaning from the idea of compromise inherent in the nautical usage.

C

Caboose The seaman's name for the galley or cook house on a small vessel, often resembling a sentry box in shape; it was located on deck, rather than between decks as in larger vessels. Sometimes called a "cuddy," although in larger sailing ships a cuddy was generally the compartment where the officers had their meals. *Caboose* is from the German *kabuse,* a small hut or dwelling; hence the usage in the United States meaning the last wagon on a goods train, which accommodated the guard, the brakesman, and any chance passengers; what the English would call the "guard's van."

On American whaling ships in the early nineteenth century, *caboose* was also the word for the try-works, the very large iron pot set up on deck for boiling down whale blubber; a variation of this was *cambouse.*

Cannon
A loose cannon A loose cannon on board a sailing ship is a very dangerous object indeed; given its great weight and mass, a cannon that has come adrift of its tackles (the ropes that control it and secure it to the ship's sides) during heavy weather presents a serious threat to the safety of the vessel and to life and limb of the crew. It could quite easily crash through the side of the ship (if it were a cannon from one of the lower decks, this would open a large breach close enough to the waterline to put the vessel in danger of foundering). To somehow bring it under control calls for extraordinary luck

and seamanship on the part of the crew.

Metaphorically, a loose cannon is a person who happens to be in possession of certain knowledge, facts, information, etc., and who for any of a variety of reasons is in a position to reveal these facts to another party, thus causing commercial, social, personal, or political distress to someone or some organisation.

Careen

From the Latin *carina,* keel. To cause a ship to heel over wholly or partly on its side, so as to clean the under portions of its hull, or to carry out repairs.

Careen is occasionally used in colloquial speech when in fact *career* is probably intended: "When she heard that the store had already opened its doors for the summer sales, she careened off down the street in her car."

Captain James Cook careened his vessel HMS *Endeavour* after she was holed on the Great Barrier Reef off the Queensland coast of northeastern Australia on the night of June 11–12, 1770. A large lump of coral had broken off and become wedged in the hull, otherwise the ship would certainly have sunk immediately. Cook stemmed the inrush of water by fothering his ship. Fothering is a method of stopping a leak by quickly stitching old yarn and rope ends across the surface of a sail or suitable piece of canvas and dragging it to cover the hole in the hull, when the pressure of water will hold the patch close to the vessel, thus allowing it to be sailed to some safe haven while the pumps are coping with the water that will inevitably enter.

Cook careened his vessel for some three weeks in the mouth of the Endeavour River, which was named by him: "To the harbour which we had now left [after the repairs], I gave the name of Endeavour River." Cooktown was some time later established on the banks of this river, close by Cook's original careenage, and named to commemorate his visit.

"He could not prevail on them to careen a single ship."

—Thomas Babington Macaulay (1800–1859), British historian and politician, *History of England* (1848)

Having got his vessel in seagoing trim again, Cook continued up the east coast, only just escaping disaster once more when the *Endeavour* was becalmed on the seaward edge of the Great Barrier Reef, the coral rampart that stretches for 1,200 miles along this coast. The late but fortuitous arrival of a breeze saved the ship and crew from being wrecked on the savage coral, and Cook decided to continue his voyage using the channels on the inner edge of the reef.

His earlier discovery, in 1770, of Botany Bay on the southeastern coast of Australia led eventually to the establishment of the colony of New South Wales in 1788, when the American War of Independence (1775–1781) made the American territories no longer available to England as penal settlements. Sydney Town, as it became known, was located in Port Jackson, some six miles north of Botany Bay, by Captain Arthur Phillip; it boasted one of the finest natural harbours in the world and the colony gradually flourished to become a major trading centre. Sydney today is still the focal point of Australian history.

Cook met an untimely death during his third voyage in 1779 when his ship, the *Resolution,* was forced to return to the Sandwich Islands (present-day Hawaii) because of problems with her foremast. The natives, having already exhausted their food supplies in entertaining Cook and his men (who were regarded as Polynesian gods, foretold by age-old legends) became sullen and troublesome. As a result of a number of misunderstandings and cases of petty theft, Cook and some of his men were attacked while ashore. In the subsequent fight, Cook was overwhelmed and stabbed to death.

"The fleet careen'd, the wind propitious filled
The swelling sails."
—William Shenstone (1714–1763), English poet, *Love and Honour,* cited in the *Universal Dictionary of the English*

Cat
No room to swing a cat

The ground-sense is of confined space; it conveys the idea that a room, house, or other area is very restricted and too small for a particular purpose. *Cat* is the sailor's abbreviation for the cat-o'-nine-tails; as a punishment, it was administered on deck, generally in the space between the poop and the mainmast. This was itself a quite restricted area, and to swing the cat effectively required some skill on the part of the bosun's mate.

To let the cat out of the bag

The cat-o'-nine-tails was traditionally kept in a bag made of red baize; naturally, when it was taken out of this bag, it was for the ominous purpose of punishment by flogging.

The expression is probably an example of the sailor's penchant for grim humour, with an allusion to the fact that a domestic cat kept in a bag is usually a flailing ball of fury when let out. Hence, "to let the cat out of the bag" was to put an unpleasant state of affairs into motion. The metaphor carries much the same meaning in colloquial speech: to allow a secret to escape, to disclose information, usually unintentionally.

The expression may also owe something to the old practice of fraudulently selling a cat trussed up in a bag as a suckling pig; the noises made by both animals in their confinement were presumably similar. If the buyer opened the sack, he literally let the cat out of the bag, and the trick was disclosed. A blind bargain such as this is known as "buying a pig in a poke."

Cat-o'-nine-tails

"You dread reformers of an impious age,
You awful cat o' nine tails, to the stage."

—*Prologue to Yanbrugh's False Friend*, cited in the *Universal Dictionary of the English Language* (1897)

A nine-lashed whip widely used for flogging seamen on the bare back in the old days of sail. The cat-o'-nine-tails was made of nine lengths of cord, each about 18 inches long, some with three knots at the end and others with a single knot worked into the cords, usually at different distances (nine cords each with a knot at the very end would present a formidable mass after only a few lashes, and could do too much damage to the seaman's back). All the cords were seized to a thicker piece of rope that served as a handle. This

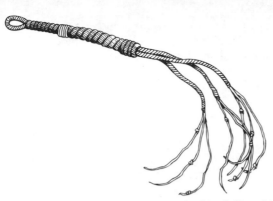

handle was often painted red, and the cat was kept in a bag made from red baize.

Curiously, most ships' cats were works of art, considered solely from the point of view of design and workmanship. They weren't just a few bits of rope tied together for the purpose of hitting someone with—rather, many of them were beautifully crafted examples of fine ropework on which the seaman could exercise his skill and ingenuity during his time off-watch.

Very often the lash used for punishing cases of theft on board was a sturdier and more utilitarian device, usually with more than one knot to each cord and larger and harder ones at that, reflecting the seaman's abomination of this crime in a shipboard society that threw so many men together for long periods of time. It was common, too, for a dozen lashes from this "thieves' cat" to be given at the beginning and at the end when a seaman was punished by running the gauntlet.

Regulations in the British navy limited the rigour of a captain to award up to 12 lashes, but this was so frequently abused that, as in *Hamlet,* the custom was more honoured in the breach than in the observance. On occasion, as many as 500 or 600 lashes were awarded for crimes that were insufficiently serious to attract the death penalty. If this seems a savage state of affairs, one must remember that malefactors in the army of that day could be given as many as 1,500 lashes.

Curiously enough, virtually all seamen approved of the cat and of the naval system of discipline in general. They knew that the ship where discipline was lax was likely to be a real "hell-ship" where everybody suffered, regardless of who was innocent and who was guilty. The cat was officially abolished in 1879. Colloquially, *cat-o'-nine-tails* could be a description of a particularly scathing or savage argument or verbal attack by one person on another.

Chock–a–block Describes the position when two blocks (or "pulleys," in landlubber's terms) have come together so that no further movement between them is possible. Technically, this is "choking the luff" of each block, whence the term *chock-a-block* derives (from *choke-the-block,* also found as *chock and block).* To increase the distance between these blocks is to "overhaul" them.

Chock-a-block is also a slang term meaning full up, to be bored or fed up, to be unable to take any more. Also, to be "chockers," a very common colloquialism in Australia.

Chunder *To chunder* is to vomit. It is widely used in Australian colloquial speech and is said to derive from the fact that a seasick passenger on an upper deck would (it was hoped) cry out "Watch under!" as he leant over the rail while succumbing to the rigours of sea travel. *Chunder* is the laconic shortening of an otherwise heartfelt cry.

Clap Originally the sailor's word for venereal disease; now a widely used colloquialism for any form of VD, but especially gonorrhea; from the old French *clappoir, clapier,* brothel.

Close quarters
To be at close quarters

"Close-quarters" were strong, very sturdy barriers of wood set across the decks of sailing merchant ships. They had loopholes cut into them through which muskets could be fired to repel or fight off boarding attacks from pirates. The essence of the phrase *to be at close quarters* is that one is closely confined, shoulder-to-shoulder, with one's fellows, with the enemy only a short distance away, all fighting furiously for possession of the deck. Colloquially, *to be at close quarters* carries with it the same nautical meaning of direct and close contact, often in a small, cramped place or position.

Coast

The land immediately bordering the sea; the seaside. From the Latin *costa,* rib, side, in the sense that the coast or shore resembles a long strip or rib, a narrow band between the sea proper and the hinterland; what geographers call the "littoral." We recognise the Latin source in *costal cartilage,* the cartilage that connects the ribs to the sternum.

The coast is clear

Probably from the days of smuggling; if the coast was clear, the implication was that there were no coast guards or revenue and excise agents about who might otherwise interfere with the smugglers' activities. The phrase carries a closely similar figurative meaning: there is no apparent likelihood of interference, there is no enemy in sight.

To coast along

"... coasting upon the South Sea."

—Edmund Spenser (?1552–1599), English poet, *View of the Present State of Ireland* (1596)

To coast is to sail along the line of the coast; also "coasting," or navigation along a coast by reference to landmarks. A "coaster" is a vessel that plies between the harbours of a particular coast or adjacent coasts, usually in pilotage waters and seldom out of sight of land (older readers may recall John Masefield's "Dirty British coaster with a salt-caked smoke-stack"). Such vessels generally encountered few serious obstacles to a safe passage, since they were always within sight of land and therefore could fix their position with great accuracy. In bad weather, such a vessel could readily put into a nearby haven.

Colloquially, then, *to coast along* is to carry out a task with minimal effort, without unnecessary fuss or bother.

Cockpit

"Can this cockpit hold The vasty fields of France?"
—William Shakespeare (1564–1616), *Henry V,* act 1, chorus

Originally, the "cockpit" in a man-of-war was the compartment under the lower gundeck where the wounded were attended to during battle. This space was near the after hatchway and was at one time used as the mess for certain of the officers on board.

Nowadays the cockpit is the well or sunken recess of a small sailing vessel where the steering wheel or tiller is located, the place from where control is exercised. Nowadays it is also the pilot's space in an aeroplane and the driver's seat in a racing car. The "cockpit" was also the pit used for cockfighting; the "pit" (or "pits") in the theatre also takes its name from this source.

Colours
To come in with flying colours

Colours is the name given to a vessel's national flag flown at sea. It is the means by which ships establish their nationalities. Such flags are of particular significance and importance to all maritime nations, and there are long-established customs and expectations regarding the flying of ensigns, national flags, and courtesy flags.

Sailing navies relied primarily on flags, not only for means of recognition, but also for the transmission of signals, orders, and the like. In battle a ship signified surrender by lowering its colours; a ship or fleet that had been victorious would sail into port with all flags flying at the mastheads. Colloquially, the phrase means to be completely triumphant, to win hands down.

To show one's true colours

To reveal one's true character, shorn of all falsehood. The *colours* is the name given to the national flag flown by a ship at sea. During the days of fighting sail, it was a common *ruse de guerre* for one vessel to fly some other national flag when being challenged by a vessel of unknown nationality. Naval men-o'-war always revealed their true colours at the moment of going into battle, but it was not unknown for some privateers to continue to sail under false colours for purposes of deception.

Cot
A cot case

A cot (from the Hindi *khat,* bed) was a ship's bed made of canvas stretched on a wooden frame and slung like a hammock from the deck beams; it was about six feet long, two feet wide, and one foot deep, with a mattress in the bottom. It often had enclosing curtains and was used by officers before the introduction of permanent bunks and cabins. It must be remembered that, in the days of fighting sail, cabins were only temporary affairs, being divided from each other only by canvas screens or removable wooden bulkheads (the sailor's term for walls). In time of emergency, such as fire or battle, they could be quickly dismantled to provide space for movement, such as working the great guns.

Admiral Nelson's cot on HMS *Victory* was slung between two guns in the stern. Despite his many years at sea, he always experienced seasickness for the first few days on board ship; his recourse was to take to his cot until the illness wore off (because of the way in which these cots were slung from the deck beams above, they remained relatively stable even though the vessel might be rolling considerably).

Colloquially, a "cot case" is someone who is ill or exhausted or in some way quite incapacitated, and who must be confined to bed to recover. Such was the case with sailors who contracted scurvy, before the days of antiscorbutics.

CQD

The original radio distress call made by a ship requiring assistance; it was introduced early in 1904 (the form "SOS" became the international signal of distress in 1908). "CQ" was the call-sign for "all stations," and "D" stood for "distress"; the signal soon became popularised as "Come Quickly, Danger."

Crackerjack A sea dish consisting of preserved meat or soup, mixed with broken ship's biscuit and other ingredients; other dishes well-known to the seafarer were "burgoo" (boiled oatmeal porridge seasoned with salt, sugar, and butter, and said to derive from the Vikings); "dandyfunk" (broken ship's biscuit and molasses); "lobscouse" (a stew consisting of salt meat, potatoes, broken ship's biscuit, onions, and available spices); and "sea pie" (a favourite, consisting of meat and vegetables layered between crusts of pastry).

The generic word for these odds and ends of food leftovers was *manavlins,* of unknown origin and variously spelled. From its earliest nautical meaning of tidbits of food, it came to mean small matters, extra fresh food belonging to whale-fishers, any small object, and the odd change remaining at the end of the day in the railway booking office (recorded in 1887). The word is used in its earliest sense by Rolf Boldrewood in his Australian classic *Robbery Under Arms* (1888).

The colloquial meaning has changed considerably. *Crackerjack* (sometimes written "crackajack") now refers to a person of marked ability, or something exceptionally fine, or to some event of note.

Cracking
Get cracking A colloquialism meaning "get busy," "hurry!," "start the job right away." From the days when mail-ships (or "packets," as they were usually called) had a penalty clause written into their contracts for late delivery of the mails. These vessels would crack on all possible sail to meet their contractual requirements; the expression comes from the fact that a

mail-ship in a hurry would set all sail such that the canvas and rigging were taut and (nearly) cracking under the strain.

Cranky

"In the case of the Austrian Empire the crank machinery of the double government would augment all the difficulties and enfeeble every effort of the State."

—*Times of London,* November 11, 1876

A vessel that is "crank" is one that lists (leans to one side or the other) easily, one that is not stable under canvas. The condition might be due to her construction, bad stowage of cargo or ballast, or a combination of any of these. Colloquially, *to be cranky* is to be ill-tempered, out of sorts, unsteady, out of order. Ultimately derived from Anglo-Saxon cranc, something bent (the modern term *crank handle* is from the nineteenth century).

Crib

"In a cryb was he layde."

—*Towneley Mysteries,* cited in the *Universal Dictionary of the English Language* (1897)

The small, permanent sleeping berths once found in packet-boats, the vessels that carried mails and passengers between nearby ports on a regular basis. Such a vessel was originally known as a "post-bark" or "post-boat." Currently, any compact sleeping berth in a small vessel is known as a "crib." Also a stall, pen, or fodder rack for cattle; now widely used to describe a child's bed or cot, usually oval in shape and made of wickerwork. Various other meanings also attach to this word. From the Anglo-Saxon *cribb,* ox-stall.

Crimp
To crimp someone's style

"Coaxing and courting with intent to crimp him."

—Thomas Carlyle (1795–1881), English essayist, cited in the *Universal Dictionary of the English Language* (1897)

A crimp is a person who shanghais or kidnaps seamen and delivers them aboard a vessel that is short-handed and about to sail. The word is related to the Danish *krympe,* to shrink, and refers to the coercion and swindling that was practised upon the unsuspecting seaman who was about to be shanghaied. The phrase *to crimp (or cramp) one's style* means to hinder or obstruct.

Cut
To cut in; cutting in

An old term from the days of whaling. The dead whale was cut up alongside the vessel by men working from the "cutting stage," a platform of planks slung outboard of the ship's rail. This job, also known as "flensing," was a very dangerous one, as the sea was usually alive with sharks attracted to the kill, and the vessel was at the mercy of the weather, making it liable to roll alarmingly during the process of cutting in. As a metaphor, *to cut in* means to interrupt.

To cut out Originally a nautical term used to describe the action of deliberately singling out an enemy ship and by various means separating her from her companions, so as to engage her with gunfire and, ultimately, to board her. Used in everyday speech with essentially the same meaning: to oust, to remove, to separate, as in the operation of cutting the wethers out from a flock of sheep. An extended meaning is "to cut it out," stop, cease, bring to an end.

D

Davy Jones   In nautical mythology, Davy Jones is the spirit of the sea, usually cast in the form of a sea devil. Thus, the bottom of the sea is called "Davy Jones's Locker," the final resting place of sunken ships, of articles lost or thrown overboard, and of men buried at sea. It is the sailor's phrase for death, as in "He's gone to Davy Jones's Locker" when referring to anyone who has been drowned or buried at sea.

   The reason for the choice of name is unknown; it is certainly reminiscent of the prophet Jonah (also known as Jonas), who brought misfortune upon the crew of the ship in which he was fleeing to Tarshish to escape God's wrath. Another suggestion is that Davy is a corruption of the West Indian word *duppy,* devil, or that Davy Jones was once a pirate. Hampshire, in *Just an Old Navy Custom* (1979), states that *Davy Jones* is from "Duffy" Jones, *duffy* being an Old English word for ghost; the phrase thus means "ghost of Jonah."

Deadwood   The name given to the blocks of timber attached to the keel fore and aft, to form the upward extensions of the keel to the stemson and sternpost. Its primary function is to build up the ends of the keel so that other structural timbers may be securely located. The deadwood pieces in themselves add little, if any, strength to the hull; hence their name. In a similar sense, the term is used to describe anyone who is a nonproductive member of, say, a business firm or a sporting team, someone who isn't contributing to the overall success of the enterprise. *To get rid of the deadwood* would be the goal of a shakeup or a review of personal performance.

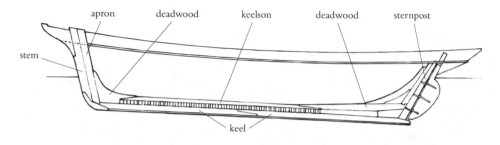

apron deadwood keelson deadwood sternpost

stem

keel

Debacle

"They could have been transported by no other force than that of a tremendous deluge or debacle of water."

—William Buckland (1784–1856), English religious scholar and geologist, *Reliquiae Diluvianae* (1823)

Surprisingly, of nautical origin; the word first referred to the breaking-up of ice on a river or navigable channel. From the French *debacle,* to clear, unbar; from *de,* away, from, plus *bacler,* bar, and ultimately from the Latin *baculus,* staff, crossbar. The word achieved widespread military use ("The enemy troops were crushed in a series of debacles from which they never recovered") as a result of the publication of Emile Zola's novel *La Débâcle* (1892). More generally, the term now means a breakup or rout, a sudden overthrow or collapse; overwhelming disaster.

Deep

"The goddess spoke: the rolling waves unclose:
Then down the deep she plung'd from whence she rose."

—Alexander Pope (1688–1744), English poet and essayist, Homer's *Iliad* (1720)

An area of ocean of exceptional depth when compared to adjacent areas; depths of over 3,000 fathoms are given the generic name *deeps.* The word was originally used to refer to that part of the ocean as opposed to the shallows near the shore. It is found in a number of figures of speech: "That new treasurer is a deep one"; "to take a deep breath"; "to be in deep sorrow"; "deep in thought"; and so on. *To be in deep water* is an obvious nautical allusion, meaning to be in trouble or difficulties. From the Old English *deop,* deep.

Deep six   To *deep six* something is to heave it overboard, usually because it is no longer of any use. As a landsman's metaphor, it means to bury or get rid of someone or something (the traditional depth of a grave being six feet): "The washing machine finally gave up the ghost after 15 years of service, so we gave it the deep six at the dump last week."

The origin of the term is the leadsman's cry as he heaves his lead to determine the depth of water beneath his vessel. The hand lead line is marked in fathoms at certain intervals with bits of cloth, leather, duck (canvas), or cord; even at night the experienced leadsman can recognise each mark and call the correct depth (sounding) accordingly. The unmarked fathoms between the marks on the lead line are called "deeps"; if the lead is heaved and it comes to rest where there is no distinguishing mark on the line, the leadsman refers to the nearest mark that he can see above the water, and calls out to the officer of the watch "Deep—" followed by the observed mark above the water. (Readers will be familiar with the significance of "mark twain," the name of the two-fathom sounding adopted by Samuel Clemens, the American writer, as a memento of his days as a river pilot on the Mississippi.)

A cry of "Deep six!" would mean that the vessel was lying in between five and six fathoms of water; the pragmatic seaman, ever conscious of his own proximity to eternity, saw "deep six" in a far more personal light, hence the significance of the expression.

Demure   Now meaning sedate, modest, decorous, as applied to a person's behaviour; but the word is of nautical origin, once used to describe the sea, to mean quiet, settled, untroubled. From the Anglo-French *demurer,* to stay.

Derelict

From the Latin *derelictus,* that which is forsaken entirely; any vessel abandoned at sea, for whatever reason. However, if any live domestic animal, such as a cat or dog, is on board when the vessel is found, the owner is legally entitled to recover the ship within a year and a day if he is willing to pay salvage. The sense of abandonment, neglect, and dilapidation is preserved in the colloquial use of the term; a derelict is a person who is completely down and out, on the skids, forsaken by society; usually occasioned by liquor.

Devil
Between the devil and the deep blue sea

To have no real choice; to be placed between two alternatives, each of which is equally precarious or hazardous. To move toward either is to invite disaster.

The devil was the outermost seam on the deck, in the waterways against the vessel's side or bulwark; it was so called because it allowed almost no room for the seaman to hammer the caulking in to make the seam watertight. It is also the name of the garboard seam, the seam between the keel and the first plank (called the garboard strake). The garboard seam was also an extremely difficult one to caulk; it was very awkward to get to, and was usually too wet to caulk properly with oakum and hot pitch.

From the point of view of the sailor, all that lay between disaster and his present position was the thickness of the planking that stood between the devil on the deck and the sea alongside. He also had to rely on the integrity of the garboard seam, it being so difficult to maintain properly at any time. In both instances, the "deep blue sea" was the inevitable dire result if the sailor neglected to carry out the necessary and always difficult task of keeping the devils in good order.

The devil to pay

The term *to pay* means to caulk a seam; to force oakum into it and cover it with hot pitch. *To pay the devil* referred to the

very awkward or difficult task of paying the outermost seam **37**
on the deck; it always generated trouble of one kind or
another. Colloquially, the phrase means to be confronted
with a situation so difficult that no means of solving it can
easily be found. It also has an extended and related meaning,
implying that if one persists in pursuing a particular course
of action there will be trouble: "the devil to pay."

Dingbat

"They ought to have put him
away in Callan Park with the
other dingbats."

—Sumner Locke Elliott (1917–1991),
Australian novelist, playwright, and actor,
Water Under the Bridge (1977)

Also "dingbats." A sailor's slang term for a mop made out of
old rope-ends and used for swabbing the deck and other
areas. The origin of the phrase is obscure; it is used today to
describe a condition of being rather eccentric or
uncontrolled in speech or actions, to be silly or dopey. In
Australian slang, it is also a term for delirium tremens. The
allusion is probably to the more or less uncontrollable
teased-out fag-ends of rope being slapped around by the
action of the mop. American usage is similar: the reference is
to someone who is flighty and foolish, especially a woman.

It is revealing of our values that the English language
contains a disproportionately large number of slang terms
that describe the wit—or, rather, the lack of it—in our
fellow man. American slang, for instance, employs more than
200 expressions for people who are supposedly a bit less
sane than ourselves, from "airbrain" to "potatohead,"
"chucklehead" to "gump," and "goney" to "schlemiel," with
"yo-yo," "zerk," and "zombie" bringing up the alphabetical
rear.

Discharge

"I will convey them by sea, in
floats unto the place that thou
shalt appoint me, and will cause
them to be discharged there."

—1 Kings 5:9

From the Old French *descharger,* to unload, and originally
used in that sense to mean the act of unloading a ship's
cargo; then used to describe the act of signing-off a member
of the crew, thereby releasing him from the obligations he
incurred when he signed on for a particular voyage or
period of service. The expression is now more widely used

to encompass the senses of letting go, to relieve of obligation, to fulfill or perform a duty to dismiss, and so on.

Ditch

The "ditch" is the sea; *to ditch* something is to throw it overboard. From the Anglo-Saxon *dic,* ditch, dike, and related to the German *teich,* ditch. As a metaphor, *to ditch* something or somebody is to get rid of, to get away from; also to crash-land an aeroplane, especially in the sea.

Dodo
Dead as a dodo

"The dodo [is] a bird the Dutch call *walghvogel* or *dod Eersen;* her body is round and fat, which occasions her slow pace."

—T. Herbert, *Travels,* cited in the *Universal Dictionary of the English Language* (1897)

The dodo was a large, clumsy, flightless bird, about the size of a goose but with small, useless wings, that once inhabited the islands of Mauritius, Reunion, and Rodrigues, in the southwestern Indian Ocean. It was very easily captured by sailors and was used by them as food; the bird's complete lack of fear consequently led to its becoming extinct in the late seventeenth century. The word *dodo* is from the Portuguese *doudo,* silly. The phrase *dead as a dodo* means long since dead, forgotten, finished with, very much a thing of the past. In American usage, a dodo is a fool, a very stupid person.

Doghouse

A raised structure aft of the main cabin in a vessel; usually a short deckhouse or main hatchway that is raised above the level of the cabin top, or coachroof. Originally an American term referring to a small temporary structure built to accommodate extra people, as in a slaver ship. The phrase *to be in the doghouse* means to be in disfavour with someone; for example, during a matrimonial dispute.

Doldrums
To be in the doldrums

To be in the doldrums is to be slack, depressed, in a state of lethargy or inactivity. The term probably derives from a combination of *dolorous,* sad, and *tantrums,* bad temper.

It is closely associated with the area of calm that lies just north and south of the equator, between the trade wind systems of the great oceans. These areas were of particular significance to the crews of sailing ships, as the men were almost always reduced to a state of severe depression and querulousness because of having to lie becalmed, often for weeks on end, in torrid heat and windless conditions, searching for the fitful gusts that occasionally reached out from rain squalls. *To be in the doldrums* is to experience physical and psychological torpor; for a sailor, the effect is quite pronounced, particularly when sailing single-handed.

Doll

"They can scarcely rank higher than a painted doll."

—Vicesimus Knox (1752–1821), *Essays, Moral and Literary* (1778)

Originally a seaman's term for a woman of the ports, i.e., a prostitute, harlot, doxy, trollop, whore, hooker (curiously, the list of terms for women of loose morals is about twice as long as that for men). The word *doll* appears in sailors' ditties in the first half of the nineteenth century. The word is a diminutive of "Dorothy" in the same way that "marionnette" is a double diminutive of the French "Marie" (there is also a Scottish form *doroty,* doll, child's toy; the Dutch *dol* is a whipping-top). *Doll* was in common use to mean mistress, pet.

Now a colloquialism to mean an attractive woman, especially one who is young; the connotation of sexual looseness no longer applies. The once-popular song "Paper Doll" uses the word in its two current senses: the singer is going to buy a paper doll (toy) so that he can have a doll (girl) that he can call his own, one whom the other fellows cannot take away.

Douse
To douse the light

"Hee used to be dowssed in water luke warm."

—Philemon Holland (1552–1637), English scholar, *Suetonius* (1606)

To extinguish the lamp, torch, or lantern immediately, for whatever reason; or to drench the source of light, such as a fire, with water so as to put it out.

From the sailor's term for striking or lowering a sail hastily, often in the face of some emergency; usually rendered in the early days of sail as "douse the top," or "douse topsail." Sailors still use the expression "douse the glim," meaning turn down or put out the lamp or light. From the Dutch *doesen*.

Drift From *drive,* which comes to us from the Anglo-Saxon *drifan,* to convey the central sense of active movement.

Do you get my drift?

"We know your drift...."
—William Shakespeare (1564–1616),
Coriolanus, act 3, scene 3

"Drift" is the distance a vessel makes to leeward as a result of the action of tide or wind, or both, on the hull and superstructure. It also describes the general movement of an ocean current that is under the influence of a more or less permanent wind system, such as that produced by the prevailing westerlies in southern latitudes.

"In the mean time, against thou shalt awake, Shall Romeo by my letters know our drift."
—William Shakespeare (1564–1616),
Romeo and Juliet, act 4, scene 1

The colloquial allusion is the direction that a person would seem to be taking when advancing an argument or explanation; one's "drift" is more by way of hint and ellipsis than by direct example or approach, as if to emulate the gradualness of a vessel's movement when drifting. Found in such metaphors as "Do you get my drift?" (Do you understand the aim of my argument?).

Duck up When the helmsman of a square-rigged vessel had his forward vision obstructed by the sails, the order "Duck up the clew lines" was given, and the lower corners (the clews or clues) of the mainsail and foresail were hauled up to their respective yards until the man at the wheel was able to see ahead properly. Colloquially, the phrase has variations: "duck up," "duck down," "duck over," etc. They all mean approximately the same thing: to go (or move) quickly, without fuss, to get something or improve matters.

Dutch From the Middle Dutch *Dutsch,* and the German *Deutsch,* denoting the people of Germany, those of Teutonic stock; it also referred to the language spoken by them. The word derives from the Old High German *diot,* people, and is related to the Old Irish *tuath,* people. It is a word from the eighth century, but from about 1600 it tended to be restricted to describing the inhabitants of what is now called Holland or the Netherlands.

As a result of the Anglo-Dutch wars of the seventeenth century, fought almost entirely at sea, the English seaman coined a wide variety of phrases that depicted the Dutch in a less than flattering manner. Some such phrases are:

Double Dutch: Gibberish, jargon, as the Dutch tongue was to the English sailor.

Dutch bargain: A bargain settled over drinks.

Dutch comfort: Cold comfort; of almost no consolation at all.

Dutch defence: A sham defence.

Dutch nightingales: Frogs.

Dutch treat: To pay for oneself; "to go Dutch."

Dutch wife: A bolster used originally in the Dutch East Indies for resting the limbs in bed; a poor substitute for the real thing.

Dutch-built: Broad and bluff, without grace.

I'll be a Dutch Uncle: From the Dutch *baas,* originally uncle, now boss or master; an expression of great disbelief, the same as "I'll be a Dutchman."

I'll be a Dutchman: An expression of surprise and strong rejection; incredulity.

To be in Dutch: In trouble, out of favour.

The word *bumpkin* (a derivative of the nautical *boom* plus the addition of *kin,* a short boom) colloquially means awkward country yokel, fellow. Etymological research suggests that it was first applied to Dutchmen.

Easy
An old nautical term, meaning to go or haul carefully, slowly, or less vigorously; to gently slacken; in general, to take the pressure off, as in easing the sheets to reduce the pressure of wind on the sail, in order to reduce the angle of heel. The metaphor, often expressed as "to ease off," carries much the same ground sense: to reduce severity, tension, or pressure so as to make something less painful or burdensome.

To take it easy
From the order *Easy!*, meaning to lessen the effort being put into a particular action; also, to take some care. Often used as an opposite of *handsomely,* which means with great care, slowly, to not lose the strain. The essential element of "easy" is to relax without actually abandoning one's duty or position. In the Royal Navy, a short break during working hours is called a "stand easy."

Exonerate

"Vessels which afterwards all exonerate themselves into one common ductus."

—John Ray (1627–1705), English naturalist, *Wisdom of God Manifested in the Works of Creation* (1691)

From the Latin *ex-,* out, from, and *onus,* burden; hence, to unburden. Curiously, it was first applied in a literal sense to operations such as the unburdening of a ship, that is, the unloading of its cargo. This is a very early usage; it has now long since meant only to clear of blame, to relieve as from an obligation, and it has quite lost its literal sense of a physical unburdening.

Eye
All my eye

The phrase in full is "All my eye and Betty Martin." It means nonsense, rubbish, without any foundation in fact. The colloquial usage is quite well known, but its origin is obscure. It is usually explained as a corruption of *O mihi, beate Martin* ("O [grant] me, blessed [St.] Martin"); originally a prayer or invocation offered by sailors of Catholic nations to St. Martin, usually in time of battle. The colloquialism is frequently shortened to "all my eye."

To turn a blind eye

To pretend not to see or notice something; to overlook a small indiscretion. Said to originate from Lord Nelson's celebrated act of putting his telescope to his blind eye at the Battle of Copenhagen in 1801, when Admiral Parker signaled Nelson to break off action. Nelson disobeyed the order, saying at the time that because he had a sightless eye he had a right to be blind sometimes.

Horatio Nelson (1758–1805), first Viscount and British vice admiral, perhaps England's best-loved and certainly most famous seagoing commander, joined his uncle's ship HMS *Raisonnable* at the age of 12. After a variety of experiences at sea, including service in the West Indies, the East Indies, and the Arctic, Nelson was made lieutenant at 19. He fought in the American Revolution (1775–1782) and was made post captain at the astonishingly young age of 21.

In 1787, Nelson was put on half pay because of the greatly reduced needs of the peacetime navy; he endured this for five years, until the war with Napoleonic France began in 1793 and Nelson went back to sea, this time in command of HMS *Agamemnon*. It was during this period that he was blinded in the right eye.

While Nelson was attacking the Danish fleet, the commander of the British squadron, Admiral Sir Hyde Parker, signaled for Nelson to break off the action. Because his ships were in a dangerous situation in shoal waters, however, Nelson refused even to see the signal, and continued his attack. As a result of his actions in this engagement, and because of his adroit handling of the armistice terms with Denmark, Nelson was made commander-in-chief in Parker's place, who in turn was recalled to England.

Viscount Nelson became commander of the Mediterranean Fleet in 1803 as vice admiral of the Blue, with his flag on HMS *Victory*. Two years later, on October 21, 1805, the great battle for which Nelson seemed to have been preparing himself all his life unfolded off Cape Trafalgar, on the southwestern coast of Spain, where he met and defeated the Franco-Spanish fleet under the command of Napoleon's admiral, Comte de Villeneuve (Pierre Charles Jean Silvestre, 1763–1806).

This engagement, known as the Battle of Trafalgar, in which Nelson himself was mortally wounded on the quarterdeck of the *Victory* by a French sharpshooter's bullet, annihilated the French forces and gave England almost total control not only of the English Channel but also of the Mediterranean. This was also perhaps the last great fleet encounter of the classic days of sail.

It was during this momentous battle that Nelson hoisted the most famous signal in British maritime history. Lieutenant John Pasco was Nelson's signals officer on the *Victory* at the time. As the British fleet sailed into action, Nelson turned to Pasco and said, "Mr. Pasco, I wish to say to the fleet, 'England confides that every man will do his duty.' You must be quick, for I have one more signal to make, which is for close action." Pasco asked if he could use "expects" instead of "confides," because "expects" already had its own signal flag, whereas "confides" would have had to be spelled out with eight extra hoists. "That will do; make it directly," replied Nelson, and thus this famous signal was hoisted (quoted from Kemp's *The Oxford Companion to Ships and the Sea,* 1976).

F

Fagged
To be fagged out

A fag-end is the unwhipped end of a rope, which through constant use has become unlaid. *To fag out* indicates the tendency of the strands of a rope to fray out at the ends; also, *to fag* is to tease out these strands by hand.

The origin of the word is the Greek *phakelos,* bundle, by way of the French *fagot* and the Italian *fagotto;* its first meaning in English had to do with sticks, loose bundles of wood. The word and its various forms are part of colloquial speech in most English-speaking countries, particularly Australia and Great Britain. *To be fagged out* is to be weary, exhausted, tired by labour, at the end of one's patience or strength.

A fag can be a number of things. In British public schools, a fag is a younger boy who is required to perform certain services for an older pupil, such as making his toast and cleaning his shoes. A fag is also a cigarette (seamen generally were inveterate smokers, and a diminished cigarette, at the end of its life, so to speak, is literally and colloquially a "fag-end"). The fag-end of anything is the last part, the final bit, especially a remnant, as of cloth. To arrive at the fag-end of a game or a party is to get there just as it is finishing; a place can be said to be at the far or fag-end of a road or lane; and so on.

"The kitchen and Gutters and other Offices of noise and drudgery are at the fag-end."

—James Howell (1594–1666), English writer, *Howell's Familiar Letters* (1619)

"From supper until nine o'clock three fags taken in order stood in the passages, and answered any praeposter who called 'Fag,' racing to the door, the last comer having to do the work. . . ."

—Thomas Hughes (1822–1896), English lawyer and writer, *Tom Brown's Schooldays* (1857)

Faggot

A man in the British Navy who, for a small fee—money, tobacco, spirits, or such—would answer to the names of those who were absent from a ship during muster (roll call) in port. In short, a faggot was a stand-in, a hireling. The term came to be used ashore with much the same meaning. Colloquially, a faggot is a person who will do one's bidding; in the United States, a faggot is a male homosexual.

Fair and square

To be just, openly honest, straightforward. From the nautical use of *fair,* which is to adjust and adapt something until it exactly suits the intended purpose; and *square,* as in "Square the main yard"—to adjust it so that it lies at right angles to the fore-and-aft line of the ship. *To square off* or *square away* is to make everything tidy, especially items of clothing; hence, to be just right, just so, all proper.

Fair enough

A phrase very common in shipbuilding and at sea. *To fair* means to shape or adjust something until it fits the whole properly, as in placing fairing stringers along the hull; *to fair in place* is to trim or adjust something without moving it from its place. *Fairing* means to correct a vessel's plans before building begins. A *fairlead* is any fixture used to lead a rope in a required direction. Fair weather is good, favourable weather that serves the purpose; and a fair wind is a wind that will set the vessel in the required direction.

Fair, to the seaman, means favourable, unobstructed, the reverse of foul; as in a "fairway," which is the navigable channel for ships entering or leaving harbour with all obstructions, if any, clearly marked by buoys and lights. "Fair enough" is an order—an imperative—for some manoeuvre to cease as it is, to hold or secure because that is its best position, as in setting a sail or catting the anchor.

As a colloquialism, it means acceptable, passable; a statement of agreement; all is well. A very common expression throughout most of the English-speaking world to signify agreement and approval.

47

Fairway

In everyday usage, the part of a golf links between the tees and the putting greens; the driving ranges where the grass is kept short. From the original nautical usage, which referred to the navigable portion of a harbour or river, suitable for vessels entering or leaving.

Fathom
To fathom something

"The short reach of sense and natural reason is not always able to fathom the contrivance."

—Robert South (1634–1716), English cleric, *Sermons,* cited in the *Universal Dictionary of the English Language* (1897)

From Old English *faedm,* to embrace, deriving from the distance across the outstretched arms of a man of average size; this *faedm* (fathom) became the unit of measurement in most maritime countries for ocean depths and the length of rope and anchor cables. Consequently, in the colloquial sense, *to fathom something* is to investigate it, plumb its depths, sound it out. To be unable to fathom something is to not understand it.

Fend
To fend off

"Ye had aye a good roof ower your head to fend aff the weather."

—Sir Walter Scott (1771–1832), Scottish man of letters, *The Antiquary* (1816)

A back-formation from defend, which in turn is from the Latin *defendere,* to ward off, to offer resistance. All the associated metaphors contain this element of defence, for example "to fend off," "to fend for oneself."

"Fenders" are the seaman's method of protecting the sides of a vessel from being scraped or crushed by another vessel or a wharf due to the movement of the sea. They are usually portable and are taken in when the vessel is underway; used especially when coming alongside. They come in many shapes and sizes, but most commonly they are constructed from cork, coir matting, old rope, rubber tires, planks, and other shock-absorbing materials. *To fend a vessel off* is to push it off or keep it at a distance using a pole, spar, boathook, or the like, in the same way a rugby player uses his arm to fend off an attacking opponent.

48

Fetch

"Fetch me, I pray thee, a little water."
—1 Kings 17:10

From the Anglo-Saxon *fetian,* to go and bring; related to our modern word *foot.*

To be farfetched

"Like a shifted wind unto a sail
It makes the course of thoughts
to fetch about."
—William Shakespeare (1564–1616),
King John, act 4, scene 2

Fetch (from the Anglo-Saxon *fetian, feccan,* from *foet,* a pace, a step) is the term that describes the distance of open water traversed by waves or wind; the longer the fetch, the higher the waves. A long fetch produces a long sea, where there is a greater distance between each wave than there is in a short fetch. Similarly, fetch is also the distance a vessel must sail to reach open water. Colloquially, *to be farfetched* suggests that a tale or explanation is a long way from the truth or the facts.

Fiddle
To work a fiddle

To work a fiddle is to be dishonest, to cheat; as with the purser in the old sailing navy illegally selling the best of the ship's stores for his own gain, or a bosun stealing an item of gear, such as a new rope, taking it ashore secretly, and there selling it. The practices were many and devious; the losers in the long run were of course the crew, who inevitably found themselves on short rations or inferior victuals, using substandard gear (sometimes dangerously so), and so on. The expression is widely used ashore in exactly the same sense.

The nautical usage probably derives from the "fiddle block," a pair of blocks fashioned together so that one (the larger) lies below, and joined to, the other. Perhaps the idea of movement and adjustment between the two blocks suggested the slang expression.

There is also "Fiddler's Green," the sailor's paradise, where all the accoutrements to a sailor's well-being are available in plenty: public houses, dance halls, and willing ladies. It existed as a sort of sailor's concept of heaven, but it is said that a number of places ashore were closely related to this ideal.

The "fiddler," of course, is the musician, found on many an old sailing ship, who provided the music (often on a simple fiddle and sometimes on a battered accordion) for the sea chanties that the seamen sang to the heave and haul of raising anchor, hoisting sail, and so on. The expression *to work a fiddle* might derive from the sailor's constant desire to frequent these palaces of delight, even if it was only a temporary respite provided by the sometimes impossible promises of his more graphic chanties.

The word is an old one, from the Anglo-Saxon *fithele,* fiddle, and bears some relationship to the Medieval Latin *vidula* or *vitula* and to the Italian *viola;* hence our English name *fiddle* for that instrument.

Field day

"The field-day or the drill,
Seems less important now."

—Sir Walter Scott (1771–1832),
Scottish man of letters, *Marmion* (1808)

This is another of those terms widely used ashore without its nautical origin ever being guessed at by landlubbers. It refers to the activity of cleaning up above and below deck, usually in readiness for an inspection, and might involve polishing, painting, or scrubbing any of the ship's gear.

It was part of the seaman's nature to be tidy and efficient in his daily work (his life and the lives of his shipmates depended wholly on his ability to work his ship properly and with due care), and he tended to be just as tidy and efficient in his personal habits. Seamen took inordinate pride in their ship, it being a matter of great honour to them never to permit another vessel to disgrace their own when it came to matters of appearance and conduct.

Field day has gone over into colloquial English to mean an enjoyable time or a successful event or outing.

Figurehead

A carved figure, usually human (but also very often animal), fixed on the stem high in the bows, just beneath the bowsprit; earlier and more accurately written as two words, "figure head." This was because shipping registry firms such as Lloyd's and Bureau Veritas used to describe vessels in terms of their rig, tonnage, dimensions, port of registry, and so on; their type of stern (round, square, counter, etc.); and the type of head the vessel had, that is, whether it was decorated with a figure of some kind and, if so, what sort.

Thus, a description of HMS *Brunswick* (late eighteenth century) would have noted that the vessel had a figurehead (the bow had a figure of some kind attached to it); in this instance, a carving of the Duke of Brunswick wearing a cocked hat and kilt. (When the cocked hat was shot away

during an engagement in the battle known as the Glorious First of June in 1794, the crew expressed so much concern at the loss that the captain gave his own cocked hat for the carpenter to nail to the head of the hatless duke.)

The figurehead was intended as a decorative emblem that expressed some aspect of the ship's name or function. Its origin is probably both religious and personal, in a milieu where a ship was treated as a living thing. Perhaps the most famous of figureheads in the U.S. Navy was that of the USS *Constitution* (launched 1797, one of the six original frigates authorised by Congress in 1794), which in later years proudly carried at her bow a full figure of President Jackson.

Eyes were an important part of all figureheads, in the belief that the ship needed to be able to see her way across the waters. Many local fishing vessels in the Mediterranean paint a set of eyes on the bows of their vessels as an aid to seeking out shoals of fish. The religious element arose from the sailors' felt need to propitiate the deities of the sea. The forms figureheads took included lions, birds, horses, boars, warriors, swans, dragons, and saints.

Figureheads of females gradually became the most popular form of decoration, which is a rather interesting development because women were considered by seamen to be very unlucky to have on board ship. Nevertheless, a naked woman—or at least the naked upper half of a woman—was supposed to be able to calm a storm at sea, presumably because the gods of the sea were invariably thought of as being male, and therefore could be somewhat charmed and mollified by the sight of a beautiful woman.

Figureheads as a decorative maritime art have almost disappeared in the twentieth century; only a few vessels—predominantly one or two Scandinavian lines—carry a figurehead of the traditional style. Perhaps the best known figurehead in recent English maritime literature is that of the *Cutty Sark,* the famous tea-clipper built in 1869. This vessel survives, fully restored, in dry dock on the Thames. Its figurehead is Nannie the witch, in flowing garments, reaching forward with outstretched arms. The story is told in the poem "Tam O'shanter" by Robert Burns (1759–1796).

Tam O'shanter, a young Scottish farmer, had late one Halloween night come upon the young and beautiful witch Nannie and her companions dancing in a clearing in the forest. He edged nearer in order to see them better, knowing full well that, according to Celtic legend, it would be a serious matter if he were discovered spying on the cavorting figures. Nannie, however, caught sight of Tam and in a fearful rage lunged toward him; the young man, frightened almost out of his wits, leapt onto Meg, his terrified horse, and galloped for his life with Nannie in hot pursuit. Fast as Meg was, she was almost not fast enough; Nannie's outstretched hands managed to grasp the end of Meg's tail and pull it off; horse and rider then bolted for freedom through the midnight forest.

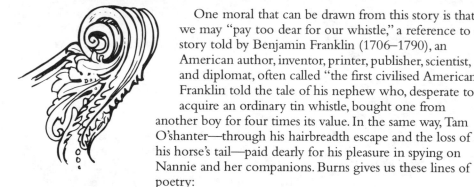

One moral that can be drawn from this story is that we may "pay too dear for our whistle," a reference to a story told by Benjamin Franklin (1706–1790), an American author, inventor, printer, publisher, scientist, and diplomat, often called "the first civilised American." Franklin told the tale of his nephew who, desperate to acquire an ordinary tin whistle, bought one from another boy for four times its value. In the same way, Tam O'shanter—through his hairbreadth escape and the loss of his horse's tail—paid dearly for his pleasure in spying on Nannie and her companions. Burns gives us these lines of poetry:

> Think, ye may buy the joys owre dear—
> Remember Tam O'shanter's mare.

Captain Jock Willis had the *Cutty Sark* built in 1869 as a challenge to the British clipper *Thermopylae;* he intended to enter the tea trade with the China coast and it was his ambition to beat the *Thermopylae,* probably the fastest sailing clipper ever built. Captain Willis also owned the *Tweed,* another very fine and fast clipper, whose lines Willis used as the basis for the *Cutty Sark.* Willis was an ardent admirer of Burns, and for the figurehead of the *Tweed* he installed a bust of Tam O'shanter, the young Scottish farmer.

It seemed logical, then, for Willis to name his new vessel the *Cutty Sark,* both for the sure, revengeful swiftness that Nannie had shown in her midnight chase and to symbolise the proud literary connection between his two vessels (you will not be surprised to learn that Captain Willis also owned the

Halloween). He had the figurehead of Nannie mounted on the cutwater, immediately under the bowsprit; it then became customary for seamen to put a piece of frayed rope in her hands, as a symbol of the fact that the ship would overtake every other rival.

It is not widely known that Captain Willis's *Cutty Sark* was not the first sailing ship to bear that name. Just before he built his famous vessel in 1869, there was another *Cutty Sark* trading on the Australian coast between Melbourne and Darwin; not much is known about her except that she disappeared in 1867, probably in one of the cyclones that occasionally ravage these northern coasts during the summer months, between November and February.

The name *Cutty Sark* refers to the short shift or shirt worn by Nannie on that occasion:

> Her cutty sark, o' Paisley harn
> That while a lassie she had worn
> In longitude tho' sorely scanty
> It was her best, and she was vauntie.

Loosely translated, this reads: "Her shift was made from very coarse Paisley linen and she had worn it since she was a very young girl; it was rather short in length, but it was her best garment and she was somewhat vain about it."

Metaphorically, a figurehead is a person who is nominally the head of a society or community; an apparent leader, but one who in fact plays no real part in leading; without real authority or responsibility, but nevertheless a person whose social, academic, or other position inspires confidence. From the fact that the shipboard figurehead was visible, out front,

54

at the head of things, attracting attention and perhaps admiration, while the real business of conducting the ship across the waters went on elsewhere.

Filibuster

"The gold-diggers and the Mormons, the slaves and the slaveholders, and the flibustiers...."
—Henry David Thoreau (1817–1862), American poet and philosopher, letter in

Filibuster is from the Dutch *vrijbuiter* and the Spanish *filibustero,* freebooter, which in 1790 came into English by way of the French form *flibustier,* and later in 1850 as *filibuster;* it is the old name by which buccaneers or pirates were originally known in Britain. Literally, it meant one who obtained his plunder or booty free.

In the nineteenth century, the term described the bands of raiders who operated out of the United States in their efforts to invade and revolutionise certain Spanish-American territories in the Caribbean. At about the same time, the phrase came into use in the United States to mean the use of obstructive tactics in the legislature, as a derivation from the original idea of raiding and blockading.

Fix
To be in a fix

A fix is the determination of a ship's position at sea by referring to any visible landmarks; by using electronic methods, such as radio or radar; or by taking sights of various heavenly bodies, such as the sun or the moon, and using tables to work out a position. A good or reliable fix was one where a number of position lines met in a small triangular space known as a "cocked hat"; the smaller the cocked hat, the more reliable the fix.

In the sense that a small cocked hat limited the possibilities for a ship to be other than in that triangular space on the chart, so colloquially *to be in a fix* is to be limited in one's ability to manoeuvre, to be in difficulties.

Flag

The word *flag* is of uncertain origin; it may be related to "flap" as an imitative sound, which in turn might derive from the Dutch *flappen,* to clap, imitating the typical sound of cloth slapping in a breeze.

"Their drowsy, slow,
and flagging wings
Clip dead men's graves. . . ."
—William Shakespeare (1564–1616),
Henry VI, Part 2, act 4, scene 1

Flags have been associated with sailing ships since the earliest times, and many nautical expressions to do with flags have evolved over the years. Some of those that have entered the language as colloquialisms are: "flag of convenience," "flag of distress," "to have the flags out," "to hoist the flag," "to keep the flag flying," "to show the flag," "to strike the flag," among others. Some of these are discussed in the following entries.

To fly the flag at half mast

It was long the custom for vessels to indicate mourning for a death on board, or for the death of a national figure, by flying the flag at half the height of its usual hoist—i.e., at half mast. This is also known as "flying the flag at the dip"; *to dip a flag* is to haul it down to the half-mast position and then rehoist it. This is the usual salute between ships at sea.

It is now a well-established custom ashore to fly the flag at half mast to signal mourning for the death of a well-known figure; this is done by governmental, semigovernmental, and commercial bodies, and often by private individuals who own a flag and flagpole. The nautical reason for flying a flag of mourning at half mast is to leave room above for the (invisible) flag of Death.

To nail one's flag to the mast

Flags are particularly important as a means of recognising the nationality of ships at sea. The earliest record of flags being used as a system of communication at sea is in 1653, when a small number of different flags were used according to an agreed scheme. *To nail one's flag to the mast* was clearly and firmly to display a ship's nationality and intentions as she was sailed into battle by a determined commander.

Similarly, as a figure of speech one *nails one's flag to the mast* when one makes it clear that a certain plan of action has been decided upon and that, come what may, one is going to do one's utmost to carry it out.

To show the white flag

Originally, the white flag was used when prisoners were being exchanged, especially by vessels that carried out the exchange between the opposing sides. These vessels—called "cartel ships"—displayed a white flag, and this became internationally recognised as the sign of a temporary truce, or cessation of hostilities. Gradually it also came to include the intention to surrender, so that *to show the white flag* now means that one party to the dispute wishes to lay down its arms and surrender.

To show the flag means to make one's presence known. In the days of empire, it was common for British warships to visit foreign ports to remind the relevant authorities that England still exercised considerable world power. The colloquial usage follows much the same intent.

Flake
To flake out;
to be flaked out

To flake down a rope is to coil it on deck in a figure-of-eight so that it will run out without twisting or kinking; often used for preparing the anchor rope or a halliard for immediate use. *To flake out* in the colloquial sense is to lie down for a rest, usually after physical exertion of some kind. The allusion is to the limpness of the body, likened to that of the loosely coiled rope (the sometimes-used alternative, "to fake-down a line," is generally unknown at sea).

American usage suggests someone who fails to do a job quite properly, either as a deliberate ploy or because of an inability to understand; such a person is regarded as being flighty, unreliable, or, in the vernacular, a "flake." Someone who is "flaky" is a bit eccentric, unconventional, perhaps even haywire.

Flannel

Sailor's slang, meaning nonsense or rubbish; often applied to a long-winded or meaningless speech. *To flannel through* is to talk or bluff one's way out of an awkward situation. Flannel is also an ingratiating manner, an insincere speech or pep talk, the equivalent of "soft soaping" someone. The slang term probably derives from the introduction of flannel material as cold-weather clothing for seamen; the comfort of the warm fabric was likened to the intended comfort or reassurance of the flattering speech: "The political candidate's address to the pensioners was a load of old flannel." Charles II decreed that, as a means of promoting the wool trade in Britain, all coffins should be lined with flannel.

> "Of all his gains by verse he could not save Enough to purchase flannel and a grave."
>
> —John Oldham (1653–1683), English satirist, *Satire against Virtue* (1681)

Flimsy

Originally a certificate of conduct issued in the Royal Navy by the ship's captain to an officer on the termination of his appointment and his subsequent transfer to another appointment. The report or certificate was written on thin paper, and the name *flimsy* derives from the word *film*. A *flimsy* today usually refers to any very thin paper, particularly the kind used by journalists when they prepare their copy for the press. A flimsy excuse is a story that one has great difficulty in believing.

> "Those flimsy webs, that break as soon as wrought, Attain not to the dignity of thought."
>
> —William Cowper (1731–1800), English poet, *Retirement* (1782)

Flog

A slang word derived from the Latin *flagellare,* to beat. Flogging is one of the oldest forms of punishment for serious crimes in the sailing navy; it was not uncommon for seamen to be flogged for quite petty offences. *Flogging round the fleet* consisted of rowing the victim alongside every ship lying in harbour, where he was given 12 strokes of the cat-o'-nine-tails by the bosun's mate on each vessel.

> "How he was flogged or had the luck to escape. . . ."
>
> —William Cowper (1731–1800), English poet, *Tirocinium,* cited in the *Universal Dictionary of the English Language* (1897)

In the Royal Navy, the law fixed a limit on the maximum number of strokes a man could receive, but some captains—known universally as "master under God"—exceeded these limits and made reputations for themselves as vicious disciplinarians. It was not unheard of for a seaman to be awarded 500 lashes, sometimes at once, sometimes in instalments. The victims usually died of bodily shock or massive infection, from the fact that the cat with its nine knotted thongs was always encrusted with the gore of its work, so that sepsis was inevitable. Flogging became less frequent after the mutiny of the *Nore* in 1797, and was made an illegal punishment early in the nineteenth century.

Colloquially, *to flog* is to sell or attempt to sell; also to steal, often with the purpose of selling the stolen item. Found also in expressions to do with speed, haste, or urgency. The connection with the nautical usage is that the metaphors preserve the sense of earnest application, of a single-minded carrying-out of a task, that was necessarily once a gruesome part of flogging on board ship.

Flurry

"The boat was overset by a sudden flurry from the north."

—Jonathan Swift (1667–1745), English cleric and man of letters, *Gulliver's Travels* (1726)

Originally, in nautical usage, a sudden squall; connected with an obsolete Old English word *flurr,* to scatter. Also used by seamen to describe the death-struggle of the whale when it has been lanced, following the initial harpooning. Now used to mean a rush of emotion or excitement, confusion or nervous hurry, as well as a light gust of wind, snow, leaves, etc.

Fly-by-night

A "fly-by-night" was an extra sail, set in the manner of a studding sail (pronounced "stuns'l"), but in a more temporary arrangement, rather than permanently. Sometimes a spare jib was used, being sheeted from the masthead to an upper yardarm. Fly-by-nights were used in the eighteenth and early nineteenth centuries. The one-horse hackney-carriage, known also as a "fly-by-night" (or "fly," for short), did not come into use until 1809, thus long postdating the seaman's use of the term.

Colloquially, a secret departure for parts unknown; also the name given to a very dubious character, one who is irresponsible and unreliable. The connection between the nautical usage and the metaphor is probably that the temporary fly-by-night sail was used when it was desired that the ship be kept moving; for example, in light airs, or—even more appropriately—in time of danger, as when threatened by an enemy vessel, a lee shore, and so on.

Footloose

Colloquially, to be *footloose* is to be free of all responsibilities and all ties, and to be able to travel about at will; a degree of irresponsibility is implied by the term, but this is not a necessary characteristic.

The expression derives from the loose-footed sail that was common in certain fore-and-aft-rigged craft, where the sail was set without a boom (such as in the mainsail of a barge). A loose-footed sail could also be set on a boom but with only the tack and the clew secured. A loose-footed sail could sometimes be very difficult to control, especially if it was not attached to a boom at the tack and clew; hence the force of the expression *to be footloose*.

Forge
To forge ahead;
to forge over

"To forge over is to force a ship violently over a shoal by the effort of a great quantity of sail."
—William Falconer (1732–1769),

A vessel was said "to forge ahead" when she was moving rapidly under a full press of canvas. She "forged over" when she was forced to sail over a shoal or bar that momentarily checked her progress. *Forge* is from the sailor's earlier pronunciation of "force." Colloquially, *to forge ahead* is to carry on with one's purpose and direction, often with renewed vigour; *to forge over* is to press on regardless of hindrances.

Founder

"The ship no longer foundering by the lee,
Bears on her side th' invasion of the sea."
—William Falconer (1732–1769),
English seaman and lexicographer,
The Shipwreck (1762)

A vessel founders when it fills with water and sinks as a result of damage or flooding; colloquially, an enterprise founders when it fails or goes bankrupt; the idea of wreck is common to both usages. From the Old French *enfondrir*, to engulf, sink.

One of the most famous founderings in history was that of the *Mary Rose*, built for Henry VIII early in the sixteenth century. In 1545, she sailed out from Portsmouth to engage the French, was immediately swamped through her lower deck gunports, and quickly sank, with the loss of nearly all her complement of 400. Her hull was discovered by divers in 1968.

60

Fraught
To be fraught with danger

Fraught is from *freight,* which in turn is from the Old German *vracht,* freight money, earnings. Whereas freight is the cargo or merchandise carried for pay, *fraught* describes the condition of being so loaded or burdened (i.e., to be "freighted with"). In the early days of commerce by sea, ships were said to be "fraught with precious wares." To be fraught with danger, horror, or the like describes a situation or event that is attended (burdened) with that danger.

Free and easy

A rope or fall (a fall is the part of the rope that is to be pulled on) is "free" when it is unobstructed, unencumbered, clear for running. A sailing ship is said to be "free" when she is sailing with the wind abaft (astern of) the beam, i.e., blowing over the stern quarters. Consequently, her sheets (the ropes and tackle controlling the sails) will be eased so as to present a squarer aspect of the sails to the wind, without undue restraint from her working gear (as opposed to tacking close-hauled into the wind, often called "flogging" because of the strain imposed on the standing and running rigging and sails). Hence the colloquialism *to be free and easy,* to be informal, casual, without restraint or hindrance; in a relaxed manner.

G

Gadget　A small device or mechanical aid or fitting on board ship used to help get things done. Often called by the seaman a "gilguy" or "gillickie." Adopted in the round by the landsman to describe things of a similar nature. Probably from *gadge,* an early Scottish form of "gauge."

Gang
To gang up

From the original usage of *gang* for crew, and also related to the meaning of a ship's full set of rigging. *To gang up,* colloquially, is to combine against, to associate together for some common purpose; to form a gang. The earliest sense of grouping together for a common purpose is still found in the fisherman's "ganghooks," on which a number of hooks are arranged in a group for more efficient striking.

Gangway
To make gangway

"I had hardly got into the boat, before I was told they had stolen one of the ancient stanchions from the opposite gangway, and were making off with it."

—Captain James Cook (1728–1779), navigator and explorer, *A Voyage Towards the South Pole and Round the World in 1772–1775* (1777)

A gangway was originally the boarded way or bridge (sometimes called the "gangboard") in the old galleys, which allowed the rowers to pass from one end of the vessel to the other, as required. *Gang* is from the Old English *gang,* alley, and is related to our Modern English *go* and to the German *gehen.*

　　In later sailing ships, the gangway came to be the platform that connected the after-deck to the fore-deck, thus allowing quick access fore and aft without the need to descend to the ship's waist. By extension, it has come to mean the movable bridge or passageway by which passengers and crew can enter or leave a ship when she is alongside a wharf or pier. The phrase is widely used as an exclamation meaning to make way, to clear a path.

Garland
Wedding garland

"Call him noble that was now your hate,
Him vile that was your garland."
—William Shakespeare (1564–1616),
Coriolanus, act 1, scene 1

A custom still practised in the Royal Navy. In the eighteenth and nineteenth centuries, British warships would hoist a garland of evergreens in the rigging to indicate that shipboard discipline had been relaxed and consequently women would be allowed on board. The garland was also hoisted on the day any member of the crew was married, and this custom exists to the present time. From the Old French *garlande,* and ultimately from the Middle High German *wieren,* to adorn.

Gasket

An original nautical word; it refers to the short rope used to secure a furled sail to its yard. When not in use, it is kept coiled, lying in front of the sail. Somehow this word was taken over by the machine age, to refer to the fibrous material used to make the joints and mating surfaces of engines tight against leakage (as in a head gasket of an automobile). The connection between the earlier nautical usage and the modern-day machine application is puzzling, but certainly the word was in widespread use at sea in the early 1600s.

The word is from the French *garcette,* rope's end; the modern-day meaning, as a joint packing, may derive from the early use of rope and asbestos fibre in making engine stuffing-boxes and propellor-shaft stern-glands steamtight and watertight. *To blow a gasket* is a colloquialism meaning to lose one's temper, usually in a sudden eruption of feeling, as a gasoline engine may blow its cylinder head gasket without warning.

Gauntlet
To run the gauntlet

Originally this was a Swedish form of punishment; from the Swedish *gat,* gate, and *lopp,* run, gate run, a lane, a passageway. In English it first became *gantlope* or *gauntlope,* the space or passageway between two files of sailors or soldiers. The expression became established in English during the Thirty Years' War, in about 1640, when *gantlope* was soon replaced by *gauntlet,* a word more familiar to English speakers.

Running the gauntlet (pronounced "gantlet" by the British and "gontlet" by the Americans) was a form of punishment that involved the whole ship's crew. The victim, usually a sailor accused of stealing from his shipmates, was made to run between two rows of seamen while they, in turn, lashed him as hard as they wished with a short knotted rope or "nettle." This punishment was known as running the gantlope or gauntlet. Metaphorically, *to run the gauntlet* is to be attacked on all sides, to be severely criticised.

> "Some said he ought to be tied neck and heels, others, that he deserved to run the gantelope."
>
> —Henry Fielding (1707–1754), English novelist and playwright, *Tom Jones* (1749)

Glad rags A term used to describe the shoregoing sailor of the 1860s, when he was given liberty to have a "run ashore," and for which he always dressed in his best and brightest clothes. Seamen, by virtue of their occupation, were extremely skillful in needlework and decoration, and they usually took great pride in their appearance when given leave to go ashore. The expression now refers to one's best clothes, worn for special occasions.

Grapple
To grapple with

Originally nautical. The word is a corruption of "grapnel" (from the Old French *grappe,* hook), usually called a "boarding grapnel," a small, four-pronged anchor often used in small boats. A boarding grapnel was heaved at an enemy vessel's rigging so that she could be held close for the purpose of boarding. Grapnels are still used today for dragging the bottom for gear lost overboard, or for the bodies of drowned persons. *To grapple with* is to seize, to hold or fasten to, as in wrestling; or to attempt to understand.

> "The gallies were grappled to the *Centurion* in this manner."
>
> —Richard Hakluyt (?1552–1616), English cleric and maritime historian, *Principall Navigations, Voiages, and Discoveries of the English Nation* (1589)
>
> "In the grapple I boarded them."
>
> —William Shakespeare (1564–1616), *Hamlet,* act 4, scene 6

Gripe

A vessel is said to "gripe" when she carries excessive weather helm and shows a strong inclination to round up into the wind. A gripe is also a lashing or fitting by which a ship's boat is secured on the deck, or on the davits, of a ship. From Old English *gripan,* to grip or seize, and related to our modern *grip* and *grope.*

Colloquially, *to gripe* is to complain constantly, to grumble about the prevailing order of things. The figure gains its force from the inherent notion of contrariness, as in the original nautical usage.

Ground
To break new ground

To weigh the anchor and lift it from the sea bed; the "ground" will be broken where the flukes of the anchor have embedded themselves. The metaphor means to commence a new project, to venture into a new area of activity; the reference is to the turning of the sod, as a new settler might do, echoing the anchor's breaking of the ground as the vessel makes ready to set off on a new stage of its voyage.

Gun
Son of a gun

Formerly a term of contempt among sailors, but now widely used in a friendly and jocular manner in Britain, Australia, Canada, New Zealand, and the United States, in all of which countries it can also do duty as an expression of surprise or astonishment—i.e., a mild expletive. It stems from the days when women—a few of whom were sailors' wives—were allowed to live on board and, occasionally, at sea. Because the working space on the gun decks always had to be kept clear and ready for action, women in labour had only the spaces between the guns in which to give birth.

A male child was inevitably entered into the ship's log as a "son of a gun," often because the child's paternity was uncertain. Such a birth gave rise to the saying: "Begotten in the galley and born under a gun. Every hair a rope yarn, every tooth a marlin spike, every finger a fishhook, and his blood right good Stockholm tar." This particular expression died out at the turn of the eighteenth century.

To bring one's guns to bear

When men-o'-war (sailing ships of the navy) engaged the enemy, they turned broadside-on so that all the guns down one side of the vessel could be brought to bear on the opposing ship, pointed and aimed for the most telling effect. The firing of all the guns on one side was called a "broadside." *To bring one's guns to bear* is a widely used metaphor meaning to concentrate one's forces—for example, the telling points of one's argument—so as to demoralise and overcome the opposition.

To stick to one's guns

From the days of fighting sail, when close engagement of the enemy meant a horrific din of ship's guns, great palls of acrid smoke, and the manic screams of excited and often terrified men. Coupled inevitably with a broadside duel with the enemy was the appalling butchery on both sides, when round shot, grape shot, bar shot, and flying splinters of wood wreaked such carnage on board that the decks often literally ran streams of blood out through the scuppers into the sea. To this end, the gun decks were generally painted red, to lessen the visual impact of the slaughter on the crew. The toll of dead and wounded was known informally as "the butcher's bill" and, more officially, as "the price of Admiralty."

To stick to one's guns, then, under these conditions, was something of an achievement (a gun crew worked a gun on one side of the vessel and a gun on the other, depending on which side the captain chose to engage his adversary). Colloquially, the phrase means to maintain one's position in spite of intense opposition.

Guzzle

"They fell to lapping and guzzling, till they burst themselves."

—Roger L'Estrange (1616–1704), English journalist and pamphleteer, cited in the *Universal Dictionary of the English Language* (1897)

To drink (or sometimes eat) frequently and greedily. Originally, *guzzle* or *guz* was the slang name in the British navy for Devonport, where it was traditional for sailors returning from a long voyage to gorge themselves on copious quantities of Devonshire cream, butter, cakes, etc. The word was in use in the sixteenth century, and it may be connected with the French *gosier,* throat.

H

Halcyon
Halcyon days

"If Anna's happy reign you praise,
Pray, not a word of halcyon
days."

—Jonanthan Swift (1667–1745),
English cleric and man of letters,
Apollo's Edict, cited in the *Universal
Dictionary of the English Language* (1897)

Colloquially, times of happiness and prosperity. *Halcyon* is from the Latin *halcyon,* and the Greek *halkuon,* kingfisher; it means "to brood on the sea." In ancient times, seafarers believed that the kingfisher laid its eggs in seaweed on the surface of the sea in mid–December, just before the coming of winter, and that because of the two–week period of incubation the waves were calm and unruffled; William Cowper used the term in this sense in *Table Talk* (1782) when he writes, "Thus lovely halcyons dive into the main." Hence the seaman's respect for and welcoming of the kingfisher's season of breeding, because it heralded the onset of good weather.

Hand

"A dictionary containing a
natural history requires too
many hands as well as too much
time."

—John Locke (1632–1704), English
philosopher, cited in the *Universal
Dictionary of the English Language* (1897).

A member of the ship's crew. From the Anglo-Saxon *hand,* and found in most other Teutonic languages; for example, Dutch and German *hand,* Old Norse *hond,* and the Gothic *handus.* Widely used in nautical expressions because of the obvious importance of having "hands" to work the ship's gear; most of these phrases have found their way into everyday usage.

Do you want a hand?

A very common expression that includes a widely used nautical term. Captain Frank Bullen, in his classic account of whaling, *The Cruise of the Cachalot* (1910), joins the crew of an American whaler by asking the captain, "Do you want a hand?" It means literally what it says: "Do you need another crew member?" Colloquially, the expression means "Do you need any help?"

Hand over fist Also rendered nautically by the phrase *hand over hand*. Colloquially, *hand over fist* indicates large quantities, as in "to make money hand over fist." From the fact that a competent and experienced seaman could swarm up a ship's rigging with great dexterity; the metaphor thus imparts the sense of an obstacle being overcome with ease, or a "large amount" (of rigging) being "subdued" as it passes through the sailor's hands quickly and efficiently.

To be an old hand One who is experienced at something, well versed in a particular occupation or skill; from the common word for a seaman or a crew member. An "old hand" was, of course, a sailor of vast experience, one who knew his duty, known in the language of the day as a "prime seaman."

Hands off! It has been claimed that the origin of this expression lay in the pirates' practice of cutting off the hand (or hands) of any seaman found guilty of stealing or of drawing a knife on his shipmates.

This, of course, is a preposterous speculation. For one thing, the literature of the sea does not support the claim; for another, any seaman with one or both hands taken off is a useless article on board any ship. No captain, piratical or otherwise, would willingly feed and clothe from ship's stores a man who was unable to add his labour to the working of the ship. The idea is absurd.

It is true, however, that in the early Elizabethan navy the drawing of a weapon with the intention of striking the captain or of "causing tumult" (in the phrase of the day) was punished by the loss of the man's right hand; if he escaped hanging for mutiny, he would then be thrown ashore at the **69** first available opportunity.

The two most common punishments on board ship were hanging (for murder, mutiny, sodomy, and some other serious crimes) and the lash, known as the "cat-o'-nine-tails," awarded in a variety of ways for a vast range of offences. Other, less serious punishments involved disrating and having one's pay stopped for a period, both still practised in today's navies.

Handsome

"A light foot-man's shield he takes with him, and a Spanish blade by his side, more handsome to fight short and close."

—Philemon Holland (1552–1637), English classical scholar, *Livy* (1600)

"His garment are rich, but he wears them not handsomely."

—William Shakespeare (1564–1616), *The Winter's Tale,* act 4, scene 3

Connected with the seaman's usage of the word *hand*. The term *handsome* now means of fine or admirable appearance; to be dexterous, graceful. Originally, though, it meant easy to handle.

Handsomely means to handle something with great care, slowly, easefully, as in lowering a ship's boat, handling ropes that are under strain, or passing an injured person over the ship's side. The words *generous* and *graceful* also suit the metaphor, as in "It was very handsome of you to lend me your car."

Handy

On board a sailing ship, *to hand* means the act of furling the sails. A "hand" was, and still is, a member of the ship's crew, commonly expressed in such orders as "All hands on deck" and "All hands to the pumps." A vessel was "handy" if it was easy to handle or manoeuvre; one of the most useful tackles on board was called a "handy billy," a simple rope-and-pulley arrangement used for shifting heavy weights, especially in the ship's cargo hold. By extension, anything that comes to hand easily and that quickly and efficiently serves the purpose is said to be "handy."

Happy hour

A brief period of relaxation for the crew of a ship, or for as many as possible, consistent with the need for the ship to remain alert and efficient; said by John Rogers (see bibliography) to be a navy term from World War I (presumably Rogers refers to the U.S. Navy; it is inconceivable that the Royal Navy of that period would have permitted frivolity of any kind on board His Majesty's vessels).

Today the happy hour is almost religiously celebrated ashore by some groups of people, gathered together in a common cause (such as office workers, school teachers, and so on), who hail the end of the working week and the advent of the weekend by letting down their hair and having a few social drinks with each other.

Many bars and taverns host a daily happy hour, usually in the late afternoon or early evening, when drinks are customarily reduced in price. The yachting fraternity, especially those hardy types who cruise the Caribbean, have stoically insisted on refusing to allow this naval tradition of the happy hour to die out.

Hard
Hard and fast

A "hard–and–fast rule" is one that is inflexible, to be obeyed at all times. The term derives from the condition that a ship was said to be in when she had run aground (*fast* is an old nautical term meaning fixed, tied, immovable). The term *fast,* as in "fast asleep," comes from the same source as *to hold fast.*

Hard up

To be broke, short of money. When heavy weather conditions forced a vessel to bear off or turn away from the wind, the helm (tiller or wheel) was put "hard up" to windward to bring about the desired alteration of course to leeward (pronounced "loo–ard"). Thus, when a person is "hard up," she has to weather her personal financial storm as best she may.

Hash

Hash is sailor's slang for food; specifically, a dish of recooked meat, potatoes, and anything else available, all mixed up

"The dishes were trifling, hashed and condited [seasoned] after their way."

—John Evelyn (1620–1706), English man of letters, *Memoirs* (1818)

together; from the French *hachis,* to chop, and related to the English word *hatchet*. A hash is therefore a mess, a muddle, a mix-up: "He made a dreadful hash of repairing my radio; it's never worked properly since." It appears in expressions such as "hash marks" (service or good-conduct badges worn on the sleeve of a sailor's jacket in the U.S. Navy); "hash slinger" (a steward in the dining room of a passenger liner, or more generally a waiter); and "to hash over" or "to hash out" (to discuss, talk over, to arrive at a solution to a problem, a usage primarily from American English).

Hat
To take one's hat off to someone

A very common figure of speech, and used as a mark of praise or admiration; often rendered as "I take my hat off to you," or "Hats off to . . . " with the person's name following. Until Queen Victoria came to the throne, the only form of personal salute in the Royal Navy was that given by doffing the headgear. The naval seaman always removed his hat to an officer, and of course junior officers removed theirs to their seniors. The Queen put a stop to this because, she said, it looked ridiculous for uniformed men to be standing about bare-headed.

To take one's hat off to another person was, literally, to salute him or her, to show respect: "I take my hat off to him for the professional finish he achieved on that paving job." The expression was used by Admiral of the Fleet Sir John Jellicoe when he paid a tribute to the men of the Harwich Striking Force in World War I: "The officers and men serving out of Harwich earn and deserve all the leave they receive, and what is more, whenever I meet them I'll take off my hat and I won't expect to receive a salute in return."

Haze
To haze someone

To bully, to inflict unnecessary hardship directed against novices or during initiation ceremonies. The term derives

"Away with you! go forward every one of you! I'll haze you! I'll work you up! You don't have enough to do! If you ain't careful I'll make a hell of the ship! ..."

—Richard Henry Dana (1815–1882), American author and lawyer, *Two Years Before the Mast* (1840)

from the practice of some captains and mates of the big square-riggers, particularly in the nineteenth century, of making life on board ship as uncomfortable as possible for the crew by keeping them hard at work at all hours of the day and night, often to the extent of inventing work for the occasion. It was a method of asserting authority over the crew.

The "bucko mate" was one who hazed unmercifully with tongue and fist, and by his brutality made life a hell for the crew. The practice arose mostly in American square-riggers, because of the competition among ships to service the East Coast–to–California run, especially in the era of the gold strikes in California and Alaska. Success depended upon speed, and speed in turn often depended upon driving the crew to exhaustion, especially during the rough and dangerous rounding of Cape Horn, when sails had to be worked frequently. Many an exhausted seaman, hazed and driven aloft by fists or a rope's end, missed his footing on the yards or in the rigging and fell to his death. From the Middle French haser, to irritate, annoy. The common slang form *to hassle* may be a derivative of this old French verb.

Heads

The "heads" are the vessel's lavatory, corresponding exactly to the domestic toilet. The name dates from the days of sail, and refers to a section forward of the forecastle that was provided with gratings and served as the sailor's privy (what Dr. Johnson in his *Dictionary* calls "the place of retirement"). It derives from the fact that early sailing ships had a small deck built over the stem (the foremost structural timber of the vessel), which in turn had evolved from a similar, very strong pointed projection known in the ancient warships as a "beak" or "beak-head," so named from its shape. This beak can still be traced in the clipper bow designs of the nineteenth and twentieth centuries.

Heads was always used in the plural to indicate both sides at once, seamen being expected to use the lee (down-weather) side so that all waste should fall clear into the sea. The decking in fact was usually a grating so that the sea could assist in keeping the area clean. The name is still in use by seamen today, even though all vessels of any size now carry the modern flush-bowl toilet as a matter of course. It has found some vogue in colloquial speech ashore, especially among weekend sailors in the clubhouse.

Headway
To make headway

Similar to making leeway, except that the term *headway* implies a more positive outcome, perhaps due to a more determined and better-informed effort. Headway is the forward movement of the vessel through the water, and is a contraction of *ahead-way*, that is, progress forward. As a figure of speech, *to make headway* is to advance, to be successful in one's efforts.

Health
A clean bill of health

Said of a vessel when all the ship's company are in good health. A bill of health was a document, signed by the authorities in the port of departure, stating that no contagious diseases existed in that port, and that none of the crew was infected with any notifiable diseases at the time of sailing. A clean bill of health was thus of great importance to any vessel wishing to enter harbour. The term has come to enjoy a wide figurative usage, as to say that something is quite acceptable, that it has passed scrutiny, or has passed muster.

High
High and dry

Said of a ship that has run aground so that the tide, falling away, gradually exposes the keel; to go aground at high water is a sorry predicament, because there will be no higher tide by which the vessel can be floated free. This is the origin of the familiar phrase that refers to someone being left stranded, helpless, in a difficult position, unable to continue normally.

Himself
Every man for himself

The order given to the crew when it is clear that nothing more can be done to save the ship; it releases each man from waiting for further instructions. It would have been the last order given, for example, to the seamen and soldiers on board HMS *Birkenhead,* as it sank off the coast of South Africa in 1852.

Hitched
To get hitched

Nautically, a hitch (from the Middle English *hitch, hotch,* to raise with a jerk, and the twelfth-century French *hocher,* to lift) is a series of knots by which one rope is joined to another, or made fast to some other object, such as a spar, buoy, or part of the vessel's gear. The allusion, meaning to get married, is obvious, and it is a well-known expression ashore.

Horse
To flog a dead horse

To try to revive interest in a worn-out topic; to resurrect a matter that has, by general consent, long since been settled. It is still a widely used colloquialism taken from the language of the sea, and has an interesting background.

The dead horse is the term used by seamen to describe the period of work on board ship for which they have been paid in advance when signing on—usually a month's wages, but sometimes two. There was a custom in merchant ships where the seamen celebrated having "worked off the dead horse" (i.e., having completed the duties covered by their pay advance) by parading a stuffed straw horse around the decks, hanging it from the yardarm, and then heaving it overboard.

To flog a dead horse, then, is to expect—vainly—to get extra work out of a ship's crew while they are still engaged in working off the "dead horse." Hence the colloquial allusion to the lack of interest that is implicit in the phrase: "Doesn't he know he's flogging a dead horse trying to interest us in his daylight saving scheme?" "The Dead Horse" is said to be the only sea shanty composed and sung for pleasure; all other shanties were sung to accompany various kinds of work.

Hulk

"A huge black hulk that was magnified by its own reflection in the tide. . . ."

—Henry Wadsworth Longfellow (1807–1882), American poet,

The "hulks" were old, dismasted men-of-war vessels anchored in the Thames and off Portsmouth and used as prison ships. Originally, a hulk was a large ship employed mainly in the Mediterranean as a transport or cargo vessel. At one time, *hulk* was the name given by seamen to the hull of any ship, but this usage had disappeared by the end of the eighteenth century. The word is from the Greek *holkas,* trading vessel, and the modern usage of *hulking* (bulky, heavy, and clumsy) stems from this original reference to a heavy, unwieldy vessel.

I

Ice
To break the ice
An ice-breaker is a specially designed and strengthened vessel, built for the purpose of forcing a path through pack ice in extreme latitudes.

Such a vessel is frequently employed to prepare the way for other vessels that need to reach some distant, ice-bound objective (as in opening a lane in an ice-bound port such as Vladivostok).

Colloquially, an ice-breaker is anything that breaks down reserve or reticence, such as in one's first meeting with a stranger, or in preparing the scene so that unpleasant or unwelcome news can be imparted. Note that the phrase "It cuts no ice with me" comes from an expression of the Iroquois Indians, a tribe from the Great Lakes area of North America: *Katno aiss vizmi*—"I am unmoved, unimpressed." Not nautical in origin, of course, but introduced into English by the Americans during the War of Independence in the 1780s.

Idler
An "idler" was originally a class of worker on board ship; specifically, a member of the crew who worked during the day but did not stand the usual night watches. The carpenter, cook, sailmaker, boatswain (bosun), and painter were the usual members of the roundhouse mess where idlers were accommodated. These men had duties that took up most of their daylight hours; hence, they were

off watch at night, except of course in an emergency. They were also sometimes called "day workers" or "daymen," and were much envied by the rest of the crew.

The term expressed little or no critical attitude on the part of the crew, as idlers worked just as hard as others during their hours of duty. However, the word is now one of denigration; colloquially, an idler is a person who idles, a slacker, someone who is work-shy, habitually avoiding duty. From the Anglo-Saxon *idel,* empty, useless.

J

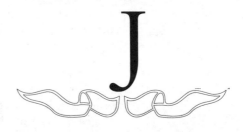

Jack
Every man jack of them

All, without exception; the whole lot; everyone. *Jack* was originally the name applied to the seamen who worked the masts and yards of square-rigged ships, as distinct from the ship's boys, but gradually it came to refer to all British naval seamen. The name is found in such colloquialisms as "Pull up the ladder, Jack, I'm inboard" ("I'm all right, Jack"), the Australian saying relating to the *Jack system,* which is the pursuit of one's self-interest.

I'm all right, Jack

From the phrase "Pull up the ladder, Jack, I'm inboard," denoting the pursuit of self-interest and complete disregard for the comfort and interests of others. Widely known as the "Jack system"; sometimes expressed as "Up you, Jack, I'm OK."

Jackknife

A knife with a blade that folds into the handle. It is tempting to suggest that such a knife was named after the British sailor, who himself was universally known as a "jack," but such is not the case. The term is an American usage, but the word itself is derived from the Scottish *jockteleg,* a large clasp knife, which in turn came from the name of a French cutler, one Jacques de Liege, who apparently invented this type of knife.

The seaman serving in sail needed a knife that was instantly available for severing seizings and other lines in times of emergency. It was carried at the small of his back, usually with the point broken off. One of the first things the mates did when signing on a new crew in the merchant marine was to break off the points of the men's knives, so as to reduce the possibility of dangerous wounds among fighting crew members. It was also a precaution in case any of the crew should later think of turning against the captain and officers.

The size of the jackknife varies; in most navies, it fits more or less within the closed fist when the blade is folded, but larger types are also in common use.

Jamboree

Now usually associated with the Boy Scouts and referring to a rally or large gathering of Scouts, national or international. The word was in use by seamen in the 1840s, however, thus predating the Scouts by some 70 years.

Originally a jamboree was a carousal, a noisy merrymaking, a spree involving singing and dancing and—when possible—alcohol of some kind. Perhaps derived from combining the English *jabber* and the French *soiree,* a social gathering, with the *m* added from the dialect word *jam,* crowd. There may also be a connection with the French *burree* or *bourree,* dance.

Jaunty
To be jaunty

"I felt a certain stiffness in my limbs, which entirely destroyed that jauntyness of air I was once master of."

—Joseph Addison (1672–1719), English essayist, *Spectator* No. 530 (1713)

The nickname in the Royal Navy for a Chief Petty Officer of the Regulating Branch, i.e., the Master-at-Arms, responsible for discipline and other police functions within the service. It is perhaps a corruption of the French *gendarme;* it might also derive from the French *gentil,* noble, genteel. The ordinary seaman often regarded the master-at-arms with some suspicion and fear, and the expression *to be jaunty* probably derives from the airs that the master-at-arms was said to assume as a result of his position of authority. It is these airs, this attitude of sprightliness and self-assuredness, to which the colloquial usage of *jaunty* refers.

Jerry-built That which is flimsy or insubstantial. Possibly the word is connected with Jericho, the walls of which, we are told, came tumbling down at the sound of trumpets. However, this derivation seems unlikely; the walls of ancient cities were of necessity built far more strongly than the story would suppose. It is more probable that the term is a corruption of *jury-built,* meaning makeshift, temporary, as for an emergency, as in "jury-mast," "jury-leg," "jury-rigged," "jury-meal," and so forth.

> "Two lumps of plaster fall from the roof of the jerry-built palace; then the curse begins to work."
>
> —*Pall Mall Gazette* (London), February 15, 1884

It may also derive from a contemptuous abbreviation of *Jeremiah,* when the Puritans were the butt of so much ridicule after the Restoration (1660); Old Testament names were commonly used among them.

The term *jerry-built* occurs in the early nineteenth century in connection with substandard building in the northern suburbs of Liverpool, a major seaport where the housing shortage was acute in the post-Waterloo years, shortly after the passing of the Beerhouse Act in 1830. This makes it far more likely that the word is of nautical origin. Etymologically, *jury* is from the old French *ajurie,* relief, help, and the Latin *adjutare,* help.

Jib The triangular foresail or headsail on a sailing vessel. Of uncertain origin, but perhaps derived from *gibbet,* the gallows (Middle English *gibet,* from the Old French *gibe,* staff). The connection is not clear. However, the word may simply be a corruption of *gybe,* from the Dutch *gijpen,* to swing from side to side.

The cut of his jib The characteristic way a person looks or acts; the art of recognising a person by, originally, the shape of his (or her) nose because of the close resemblance between the outline of the jib on a sailing ship and the silhouette of the human nose.

Sailors could recognise the nationality of other warships at sea by the variations in the shape of this triangular foresail (the jib) long before the ship's flag of nationality could be determined. For instance, Spanish ships had either a very small jib or none at all; French ships often had two jibs in a period when other ships flew only one. Other differences lay in the ways in which jibs were actually cut: French jibs had a more acute angle at the clew, thereby making it readily distinguishable from the jibs of other sailing navies.

Headsails (Jibs) of a late 19th-century sailing ship

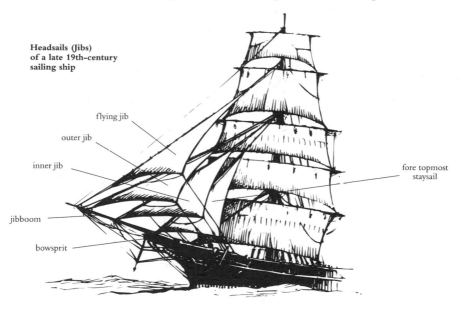

flying jib

outer jib

inner jib

fore topmost staysail

jibboom

bowsprit

To jib at something   To express alarm at something; to back out of some standpoint or enterprise; to have second thoughts. Often applied to a horse, which is said to *jib* when it is startled by something. The essential element is surprise at some unexpected development or event.

The phrase derives from the term for a nautical manoeuvre, *to gybe,* often spelled *jibe,* which means to allow the wind to blow from astern over the same side that the mainsail is set, in a fore-and-aft rigged vessel. This causes the boom and sail to swing with considerable violence to the other side, often with serious results to standing rigging or an unwary crew member. A controlled gybe is a deliberate and prepared-for evolution; it is the accidental gybe that takes the helmsman by surprise. The word comes from the Dutch *gijpen,* to swing from side to side.

Jiffy A very short period of time; in a moment, a brace of shakes. The origin of the word is unknown, but it was in use in the eighteenth century, and is part of the sailor's idiom. The word is also part of the trademark name used by Australia Post for its "jiffy bags," the strong, padded paper bags used for sending objects through the mail.

Jigger Colloquially, a jigger is a "thingamy," a "gadget," a "what-do-you-call-it," a "thingummybob," a "thingummyjig"; more exactly, an indefinite name for a thing or person that the speaker cannot define or designate more clearly. The word is from *jig,* a dance, from the French *gigue,* dance, and the Old French *gigue,* a fiddle, and finally applied to a wide variety of small mechanical devices.

Nautically, a jigger was originally a light tackle used for many small purposes on board ship, usually associated with holding or helping to haul on moving parts, such as ropes, anchors, and booms. The essence is that it was a gadget with many applications. The word was also used to name the jigger-mast, a small mast set right aft in some sailing vessels; the mizzenmast of a yawl is sometimes called the jigger-mast, and the fourth mast in a schooner of four or more masts is also named the jigger-mast.

The expression *I'll be jiggered!,* a mild oath of astonishment, probably derives from the *chigre,* known also as the "jigger" or "chigger" (French *chique,* Spanish *chico,* small), the flea–like insect in the West Indies that burrows into the skin of the feet and breeds there unless quickly removed. It is a source of great annoyance to the victim.

Jolly Roger   The much-feared flag of the old-time pirates and mutineers, on which was depicted a skull with crossed thigh bones beneath. There is no evidence that such a flag was ever flown by pirate ships as a whole; the generally recognised pirate symbol was a plain black flag, which some pirate ships were occasionally reported to have flown from their main masthead.

However, a number of particularly fierce (and therefore well-known) pirate captains did fly flags adorned with skulls, bones, and similar morbid devices, and there is no doubt that these flags captured the public's attention and served to identify all pirates with such flags.

The early eighteenth-century French pirate Emanual Wynn, for example, favoured a skull placed on crossed bones, with an hourglass below to advise his victims that time was running out; Henry Every preferred a skull in profile, adorned with headband and earrings, and crossed bones beneath. Blackbeard (who began life as Edward Teach or Thatch or Tash or even Drummond, the last according to Daniel Defoe, an early chronicler of pirate history), the man who best fitted the public's image of what a real pirate should be like, flew a flag that sported a horned devil-skeleton with an hourglass in one hand and a spear in the other. Whatever the pirate captain's fancy in flags, it was certain to convey the appropriate chilling message to his victims.

The origin of the name *Jolly Roger* is obscure. Some say it is a corruption of *joli rouge,* a French expression meaning "pretty red," a reference to the red flag often flown by privateers. Another possible explanation, however, is that *Jolly Roger* arose from the fact that from the sixteenth to the eighteenth centuries, the word *roger* in English meant to have sexual intercourse, usually of a vigorous kind, and often in the nature of rape. One of the earliest names for this flag was *Old Roger,* recorded in 1723, and even before then *roger* was a slang term for penis. It is known from the literature of the period that pirates generally treated women in a less than gallant fashion: in short, they were often bound and "rogered at the rail" by all and sundry, and then frequently thrown overboard to fend for themselves.

Junk

In the seaman's world, junk is, strictly speaking, old or useless rope or cordage. The word derives from the Latin *juncus,* a reed or rush once used in the making of cordage. The word was also applied to the salt meat that made up the sailor's staple diet, through its alleged similarity to the ends of old rope. It is interesting to note that salt pork continued to be issued in the British fleet as late as 1926. The colloquial meaning applies to anything that is fit only to be condemned; the emphasis is upon uselessness.

The Chinese vessel known to the Western world as the "junk" is so named because its sails were commonly made of reeds or rushes *(juncus).* The Portuguese gave it the name *junco,* which later went into English as the familiar word *junk*.

Jury
Jury rig

Anything that is "jury-rigged" on board a vessel is a temporary affair to replace a permanent structure that has been carried away, as in a "jury mast," "jury rudder," and so forth. The term *jury leg* is sometimes applied to a person's wooden leg. The colloquial application ashore is obvious, as in to have some jury chairs and tables—i.e., temporary or makeshift furniture.

K

Keelhaul

"The unfortunate Smallbones was to be keelhauled."

—Frederick Marryat (1792–1848), British naval officer and novelist, *The Dog Fiend or Snarleyow* (1837)

An old naval and merchant service punishment, which involved tying ropes to the hands and feet of the offending seaman and dragging him under the vessel's keel from one side to the other. (In extreme cases, the victim would be dragged from stem to stern—i.e., from the front of the ship to the back; such instances were rare and would have been used when there was no intention of giving the wretched man a chance of surviving.) The result was naturally often fatal, if not from drowning, then from laceration by barnacles, loss of blood, or the infection that inevitably followed.

A far less severe method was to pass a line beneath the vessel from one side to the other, with one end secured to the victim; tie a deep-sea lead to his feet; drop him overboard; and haul him under the ship and up the other side. The lead weight would keep him free of the barnacles on the hull (one could only hope that the operation was carried out in the sailors' usual efficient manner).

The punishment (which in the Royal Navy was not a standard form of dealing with malefactors, nor was it ever awarded by any naval court-martial) was said to have been introduced by the Dutch, who were still using it in 1813; it was certainly common in other navies between the fifteenth and seventeenth centuries. From the Dutch *kielhalen, kiel,* keel, and *halen,* haul.

Metaphorically, the phrase carries a note of dire threat of reprisal; to haul someone over the coals unless matters are quickly put right; to reprimand severely.

Kick
To kick upstairs

Originally a nautical idiom; it means much the same today as it did 200 years ago in Britain's Royal Navy. Colloquially, it is to get rid of, to have someone out of the way, by promoting him or her to a position where that person's influence is less likely to be felt.

Kickback

Any sum of money paid for favours received or hoped for; usually a corrupt practice. A nautical expression from the days when seagoing captains sought to augment their already meagre salaries by entering into a fraudulent agreement with, for example, a ship's chandler, whereby the captain would return or "kick back" a proportion of the ballast, ship's stores, or such into the merchant's stock. The value of goods thus returned would be divided between the captain and the merchant; the ship's owners, of course, unwittingly paid for the full amount as entered on the ship's papers. The practice is widespread in many areas of politics and commerce.

Kidnap

"He had long been a wanderer and an exile, in constant peril of being kidnapped."

—Thomas Babington Macaulay (1800–1859), English historian, *History of England* (1848)

The term *kidnapping* originated in the seventeenth century, when it referred to the "nabbing" of a "kid" or child for sale to sea captains, who then transported that unfortunate person to the plantations in the American colonies. Its origins were essentially maritime; nowadays the phrase embraces the capturing of persons of any age for the purpose of holding them for ransom. Another term of identical meaning is *barbadose,* which additionally meant to transport convicts to the Barbados Islands in the Caribbean in the time of Cromwell.

Kite
To fly a kite

Kite was the general name given to the light-weather square sails that could be spread at the masthead to make the most of light following winds. Included would be the moon-rakers and skyscrapers of the late nineteenth- and early twentieth-century grain ships and nitrate ships that marked the end of the great age of sail.

To fly a kite—to hoist such a sail—meant literally to see what would happen, to see whether any improvement could be made in the vessel's speed; hence the idiom, to do something tentatively (in word or deed) to test the reactions to an idea or a plan. From the Anglo-Saxon *cyta* and related to the German *kauz,* a kind of owl.

Knock
To knock down

When a cask was dismantled into its component parts—the staves and hoops—it was said to be "knocked down." Sailing ships of any size carried a cooper on board, whose duty was to maintain and repair the casks so that they were in good enough condition to carry the crew's food and drinking water. For many hundreds of years there was no other way of successfully storing the ship's provisions for a voyage of any length; hence the importance of casks as part of the vessel's equipment.

This sense of disassembly is echoed in everyday figures of speech, such as to "knock down" a vehicle or a machine; that is, to take it apart or to reduce it to its parts, usually to facilitate its handling or despatch. "It is common for some motor manufacturers to export their farm vehicles in a CKD condition—i.e., Completely Knocked Down."

To knock off

This expression means to stop work, to stop whatever one is doing. It also carries the additional meanings of to steal; to kill; to quickly compose something such as music or a poem; to deduct an amount of money from the total; and so on, but in this context it refers to that hallowed time of day when the world's workers may lawfully cease their labours and go home.

But where did the phrase come from? *To knock off* makes as much linguistic sense as *It cuts no ice with me.* In fact, there is a logical explanation for the term and it comes from the sea. It traces back more than 2,000 years to the time of the ancient Romans, when slaves spent their days (all of them) chained to the oars of the galley, busily heaving the ship from one end of the Mediterranean to the other, conveying armies or important functionaries on official business. Frequently they were also required to row the vessel into battle (and, if they were lucky, out of it; otherwise they went down with their ship).

The only way for the rowers to keep the vessel moving efficiently was to work the oars to a definite rhythm, and the easiest way for them to keep a rhythm was to have a person at the stern beating a drum or slotted or hollow block of wood with mallets to the required cadence. From time to time the rowers would have to rest from their labours, and the signal for this was a blow or a knock on a separate drum or wooden block that gave out a quite different note. This was the signal for the galley slaves to stop rowing; instead of "leaning on" their oars (still a term in rowing and boat-pulling today), they could "lean off" at the sound of the special knock or beat. It was "knock-off" time.

Knots
At a rate of knots

No sailor would ever use the expression *at a rate of knots;* the word *knot* (from the Anglo-Saxon *enotta*) already expresses the idea of rate. It is therefore rather puzzling that Captain Frederick Marryat (1792–1848), an experienced and distinguished captain in the Royal Navy, should write in one of his popular novels, *Mr. Midshipman Easy* (1836), that a vessel was "running about three knots an hour." To use the expression in this way is a tautology.

A knot is the nautical measure of speed, and is defined as a speed (or rate) of one nautical mile per hour. A nautical mile in practice is almost exactly 6,080 feet; in theory, it is one minute of arc measured on a meridian (the meridian chosen for the standard is at latitude 48°N), with the apex of the arc at the earth's centre. As a measure of speed, the expression is always just so many knots, never knots per hour; a ship may be doing seven knots, but never seven knots per hour.

The term *knot* is a direct descendant of the old chip-log (sometimes called a "Dutch log") used for centuries on sailing ships to measure the speed of their progress through the water. The log (or chip) was a flat timber about the size of a dinner plate, with a long line attached to it. This line had knots tied into it at certain intervals, which were arrived at as follows. Experience told seamen the total length of line that could be heaved and retrieved by hand, given the likely best speeds of various types of sailing vessel. It was found that the sandglass best suited for timing the operation was the 28-second glass; a glass of greater duration (say 30 seconds or more) would give a slightly more accurate result, but the much greater length of log–line running over the stern in that time would be a considerable burden to haul inboard. Thus, the proportion of 28 seconds to one hour gave the proportion of 47.25 to 6,080 feet:

$$\frac{28}{3600} = \frac{47.25}{6080} \quad \textit{or very nearly}$$

The log–line was then knotted at intervals of 47 feet 3 inches.

When the log (or chip) was heaved into the sea astern of the vessel, one seaman would let the line on the reel run out through his fingers until he felt the "start knot," which was placed so that the chip would be far enough astern to be clear of the ship's wake. He would shout "Turn!" and another seaman would immediately upend the 28-second glass. The log-line operator then kept count of the number of knots that passed through his fingers as the log-line unwound itself from the reel.

As soon as the 28-second glass was emptied, its tender would yell "Nip!" The number of knots that had run out through the first man's fingers in that period gave the speed of the ship in nautical miles per hour, otherwise simply expressed as knots. For even greater accuracy, the speed was sometimes expressed as knots and fathoms, indicating more exactly how much line had gone overboard during the timed interval of 28 seconds.

Many of the tea and wool clippers of the late nineteenth century logged occasional bursts of 15 knots or more, and some recorded 19 knots and even higher speeds. To handle a vessel at those speeds would be a hair-raising and hazardous experience indeed. The average speed for everyday pleasure sailing craft varies between four and eight knots, while offshore racing yachts consistently maintain double figures, depending on hull type and weather conditions.

L

Laid
To be laid up

"Lay up these my words
in your heart. . . ."
—Deuteronomy 11:18

To lay up is to store away, or to take a ship out of service. (In another usage, *to lay up* is to twist the strands of a rope together.) *To be laid up,* then, is to be out of action, out of commission; a person temporarily incapacitated through injury or illness is said to be "laid up," especially if confined to bed.

Land
No-man's land

The space amidships of a vessel, between the after part of the forecastle and (generally) the foremast. In this space were stored the blocks, rope, and other tackle that might be needed when working the forecastle. It derives its name from being neither on the starboard nor the port side, and neither in the waist nor on the forecastle.

The term later came to be applied to the area of land between hostile lines of entrenchments, or to any space contested by both sides and belonging to neither. More freely, it is a wilderness, a place to be avoided as dangerous.

To see how the land lies

Colloquially, to see whether things are promising or not; to see what sort of conditions one might be facing, often rendered as "the lie of the land"; to investigate a situation or a circumstance. From the days when sailing ships without adequate charts often had to work slowly in to an unfamiliar coast to navigate safely; the condition of the sea bottom and the nearby coastal terrain would be noted and recorded for future reference.

Lassie

In itself, *Lassie* is not a nautical term, but the name of this famous collie has an interesting connection with maritime history.

The first British battleship to be torpedoed by a German submarine was HMS *Formidable,* sunk just off Portland Bill in the English Channel in 1915. A few hours after the sinking, some fishermen found the body of a seaman that had been washed ashore in Lyme Bay; they carried it to West Bay and laid it out on the floor of the Pilot Boat Inn, and out of decency covered it with a tarpaulin.

However, the dog belonging to the landlord of the inn kept pulling aside the tarpaulin and licking the face of the dead seaman. Despite every discouragement, the dog persisted until the landlord was forced to see for himself what the dog had apparently known all along: that the seaman was not yet dead. The man was revived, and that is the end of his part in this story. Eventually, though, the incident inspired the famous film featuring the collie who won the hearts of millions of children the world over for her bravery, loyalty, and intelligence.

The point of this anecdote is that the dog was named after the survivor of the sinking of HMS *Formidable,* John Lassie.

Launch
To launch (something);
to launch into

"Their cables loose, and launch
into the main. . . ."

—Alexander Pope (1688–1744), English
man of letters, Homer's *Odyssey* (1726)

Deriving from the Old French *lancier,* to pierce, probably from the obvious idea that a newly built vessel, when slid or heaved down to the water's edge, then "pierces" the surface of the water so as to float.

The naming of the vessel takes place at the moment of launching, when a bottle of wine or champagne is broken on the vessel's bow. This is a remnant of an ancient custom of pouring wine over the vessel and the nearby sea as a libation or offering to the sea-gods, to appease them during the launching, that is, to placate them for the rude piercing of their domain when the vessel entered the water. The Vikings used to tie slaves onto the launching skids, so the blood from their crushed bodies spattered the hull and thereby became an offering to these sea-gods.

As a metaphor, the phrase is used in "to launch a scheme," "to launch into something," and so on; the controlling idea is to cause to move, to set going.

Lead
A lead-swinger;
to swing the lead

A very common expression, meaning to avoid duty by feigning illness or injury; to malinger. Its origin is interesting.

The term as used today is a corruption by twentieth-century military of an earlier nautical expression, *to swing the leg,* which referred to a dog's habit of running sometimes on only three legs either to rest the fourth or to elicit sympathy from an onlooker. Soldiers confused this phrase with the sailor's technical term *heaving the lead,* meaning to take soundings with the hand lead line to roughly determine a vessel's position when offshore. (Note that it is never *swinging* the lead when taking soundings—it is always *heaving* the lead.)

It was assumed by soldiers that this seaman's duty was an easy one, allowing of loafing and slacking, but in fact it is a task requiring considerable skill, effort, and experience on the part of the leadsman. The lead weight was necessarily quite heavy, about 14 pounds for the deepsea (pronounced "dip-see") lead line, which itself was 100 fathoms (600 feet) in length. Furthermore, the lead line had to be retrieved by hand, often at night and frequently in stormy conditions, during moments of considerable stress and anxiety when the vessel had no other means of immediately fixing its position. The task was anything but a sinecure for the leadsman, who couldn't have shirked his duty even had he wanted to, as the officer of the watch, and perhaps the captain and pilot as well, were often watching him closely so they could plot his shouted depths as quickly as possible.

An extension of the colloquialism means to spin a yarn, to tell a tall tale; the connection lies in the fact that the storyteller is exaggerating the facts of his yarn to elicit admiration, sympathy, or such. *Swinging the lead* is a verbal device for neglecting one's work, inventing excuses to hide the fact of one's own mistakes or inefficiency.

Leak
To spring a leak

When a seam opens up in a ship and admits water, it is said to *spring a leak*. When the butt end of one of the planks in a wooden vessel breaks loose of its fastenings and, because of hull curvature, springs outward to project beyond the side of the ship, the plank is said to be "sprung." The phrase *to spring a leak* now applies to any break or hole in a ship's hull, regardless of how it occurs, that allows water to come in. The phrase is widely used ashore, both literally and metaphorically.

Lee

From the Anglo-Saxon *hleo,* shelter, warmth. Nautically, the side of the vessel that is sheltered from the wind (as distinct from the weather side of a ship); also the direction toward which the wind blows.

To bring by the lee

Said of a vessel which, when running with the wind, experiences a sudden wind change from one quarter across the stern to the other quarter. Not a safe point of sailing, for it could lead to broaching and capsizing. Colloquially, *to bring someone by the lee* is to bring her up sharp, to cause her to be taken aback; to be very surprised and disconcerted.

Leeway

Leeway is the distance a vessel is set down to leeward (pronounced "loo-ard") of her course by the action of wind or tide or a heavy seaway. The term describes the amount of offset between the vessel's charted course and the course actually sailed over the ground, the difference between the two being the result of the action of weather and sea on the hull and superstructure of the vessel. *Lee* is from the Old English *helo* and *hleow,* covering or shelter.

To make leeway

To make leeway is to get on or to struggle effectively against odds of some kind, as, for example, in an argument or in some task requiring sustained effort. Often expressed as "Are you making any leeway?"

To have leeway means to have room to manoeuvre, especially to have space or time in which to overcome some problem. In this sense the phrase also means to have fallen behind in something, to have widened the gap between performance and objective. *To give leeway* is used in the same sense.

"There are plenty of difficulties in the road, and there is a great deal of leeway to be made up."

—*Pall Mall Gazette* (London), November 25, 1884

To make up leeway is to make up or recover the ground or distance lost by the action of leeway caused by wind or tide. As a metaphor, the expression also applies to the effort exerted in trying to make up distance or advantage lost (as in the distance in a footrace, or a student's classwork after an absence).

Leg
Shake a leg

A common expression on board, meaning "come on! hurry up! get going!," and understood in these senses wherever English is spoken.

Show a leg

A nautical expression meaning "Jump out of bed and be sharp about it!" In general, a cry of encouragement to urge someone into activity of some kind; to get on with the job. Used ashore in exactly the same way as it was (and still is) used at sea: "Come on you lot! Show a leg! It's six o'clock and the fish are biting!" From the traditional call used to rouse or turn out the crew in a sailing warship.

In the old days (until about 1840), naval seamen were refused shore leave for fear that they would desert; as some sort of recompense, women—ostensibly wives—were allowed to live on board while the ship remained in harbour.

Naturally, they had to sleep somewhere, so they joined the men in their hammocks at night.

When the crew was called to turn-to in the morning, the boatswain (pronounced "boe-sun") would check a hammock that was still occupied by requiring the sleeper to show a leg over the hammock's edge. If it was hairy, it was probably a male; if less so, probably female. By this means the bosun felt able to detect any malingering seaman.

Limey

"They would not go on a limejuicer, they said, for anything."

—*Pall Mall Gazette* (London), August 25, 1884

An American and Australian slang term for a British sailor, a British ship or—in more recent decades—a Briton himself. The name derives from the practice of issuing lime juice to British crews to combat scurvy. Vessels that did so were widely known, especially among American sailors, as "lime-juicers."

It is interesting to note that although the cure for scurvy was discovered by Dr. James Lind (d. 1794) in 1735, another 40 years elapsed before lemon juice was made a compulsory victualing issue in the Royal Navy. Lime juice has in fact only half the scorbutic value of lemon juice, and it wasn't until 1912 that vitamins were discovered and the true cause of scurvy established.

Line
To cross the line

A well-known and long-established custom at sea: *to cross the Line* is to cross the equator. When this happens, all those on board are summoned to "King Neptune's court" and are dealt with in a number of (sometimes rough-and-ready) ways designed to initiate the first-timer into the mysteries of the sea. These celebrations were a popular diversion from shipboard routine, and afforded a harmless, albeit vigorous, means of letting off steam for all concerned.

A number of King Neptune's attendants in the ceremony are designated as "nymphs" and, oddly enough, "bears," who ensure that the novices are soundly ducked in a bath after having been attended to by the ship's surgeon and barber. A certificate is then awarded, which exempts the first-timers from a repetition of this treatment on any future crossing of the Line that they may undertake.

The ceremony owes its origin to ancient pagan rites connected with the propitiation of the sea-god Poseidon or Neptune. With the spread of Christianity, many of the vows and offerings made to the heathen gods were transferred to the saints of the church. It is worth noting that the belfry, which once contained the ship's bell, was probably the site of a very early shipboard shrine; this may explain the well-established tradition of saluting as one enters the ship.

To cross the line has an additional meaning in American slang. A person who acts irresponsibly, in a way that exposes him or her to serious criticism or even danger, is said to have "crossed the line." This is a colloquial development of the original usage. To cross the line in the social sense is likened to the crossing of the equator: once done, it cannot be undone.

Lines
On (along) these lines

From shipbuilding. A ship's lines are the designer's drawings of the vessel, usually consisting of three plans: the sheer plan, which shows the hull cut vertically down the centre line and viewed from the side; the body plan, which shows vertical cross-sections when viewed looking aft or looking forward; and the half-breadth plan, which shows views of the vessel from above as it is sliced horizontally at different levels.

It was only late in the sixteenth century that ships began to be drawn up on paper; until then, ships had been built "by eye," with the shipwright's own know-how and the rule-of-thumb methods passed down from father to son. With the introduction of sets of drawings for a proposed vessel, it was possible to anticipate problems and modify designs in the light of previous experience. To build a vessel "along these lines" was, of course, to construct her according to the plans as laid down. Colloquially, the phrase means "in this manner," "in this fashion," "similar to the way I've shown you."

Listless

Originally a seaman's word to mean that there was no wind and therefore the vessel had no list on her; *listless* is a replacement for the earlier *lustless,* without pleasure. Today we use the word to mean rather the same sort of thing, as when someone feels no inclination toward, or interest in, doing anything at all; to be in a listless mood, to be bored, full of ennui.

"Hence an unfurnished and a
listless mind,
Though busy, trifling; empty,
though refined."
—William Cowper (1731–1800),
English man of letters,

Loaded

Seamen's slang meaning to be drunk. The reference was to the load marks on the side of the vessel, cited by Rogers (see bibliography) as eighteenth century, but certainly not in connection with any loading or lading marks on sailing ships. These marks were not introduced until the passing of the Merchant Shipping Act in 1876, as a result of the efforts of Samuel Plimsoll, M.P., who fought in Parliament for better conditions for seamen.

Log

A log was originally a speed-measuring device for ships at sea. Whenever the vessel's speed was measured, each log of the watch was recorded in a journal kept for that purpose. Gradually this journal became known as the "log book," and was also used to record the general proceedings of shipboard life and navigational matters. Misdemeanours and more serious offences were also entered into the ship's log, and a person so reported was said to be "logged."

To log or *log-in* means to record oneself as being present or having attended. Users of computer networks must usually "log themselves in" before they can operate the system.

Loggerheads
To be at loggerheads

To be squabbling, arguing, exchanging blows; to be in a state of disagreement over something. A loggerhead was a tool used in the caulking and sealing of seams on board ship. It consisted of a long rod with a ball of iron attached to one end (sometimes the rod would have a ball at each end); the balls were heated in a fire to red heat and then plunged into a bucket of tar or pitch to soften the pitch.

A loggerhead was also a bar-shot, i.e., a bar with a cannonball attached one at each end, and generally fired at the rigging of an enemy vessel in an attempt to cut it down. It was—along with "chain shot," "grape shot," and "langrel" (bits and pieces of iron fired in a canister)—a very effective antipersonnel device: it killed men in great numbers. The loggerhead was also a sturdy wooden bitt or stanchion in the stern of a whaling boat, with which the harpoon line could be controlled after the whale had been struck with the harpoon.

loggerhead for heating pitch

bar shot loggerhead

Because of the shape of this caulking tool, the iron spheres at opposite ends of the bar could never come together; the tool could also be an effective weapon in a fight between seamen. Hence the metaphor, to be on bad terms with someone, with little chance of reconciliation.

Longshoreman   An American term for a waterside worker, what Australians would call a "wharfie" or "lumper." From the combination of *alongshore* (at or by the shore) and *man*. Note that the British sailor of the eighteenth and early nineteenth centuries referred to his shoregoing clothes as "long clothes," which was an abbreviation for "longshore clothes."

Look alive!   An old naval and merchant service term, meaning to hurry, get going; now firmly embedded in everyday speech.

Lump sum   The sum of money paid to a "lumper," or waterside worker, when he had finished a particular job of loading or unloading a ship. The phrase today carries much the same meaning: to accept one's payment, entitlements, or such as a final payout rather than in installments.

M

Made
To be made;
to have it made

Originally, *to be made* was for a midshipman in the Royal navy to pass his lieutenant examinations and then, when a vacancy occurred, to be given his first command. This would be at the rank of captain of a small vessel; after sufficient experience, he would be posted into a rated ship with the rank of post-captain.

Until a midshipman made his lieutenancy and thence his captaincy, there was very little future for him in the navy. His prospect of a commission rested almost entirely on whether his country was at war with another maritime power. Paradoxically, the onset of peace meant hard times for these men, for they usually found themselves ashore, thoroughly skilled as seamen but totally unsuited to the occupations of city and village. The phrase has found its way into everyday speech; *to have it made* is a colloquialism meaning to be assured of success.

Main
In the main

The "main" is the old term for the ocean, the high seas, often used specifically to refer to the Spanish Main, an area of sea in the Caribbean stretching from the Isthmus of Panama to the Orinoco River on the north coast of South America. It is also an even older word for the coast of the mainland; this was in fact the original meaning of *Spanish Main,* i.e., the mainland coast that bounded most of the Caribbean sea.

102

Colloquially, *in the main* means broadly speaking, on the whole; reflecting the wide-sweeping emphasis in the nautical usage of the phrase. *Main* is derived from the Old Norse *meginn* or *megn,* strong; *mainland* is rendered by the Old Norse *megenland*.

Mainstay
To be one's mainstay

"The laws which the Irish parliament of 1703 conceived to be the mainstay of the Protestant interest...."

—*The Edinburgh Review*
(Scottish periodical), July 1857

A "stay" is a part of the standing rigging that supports a mast in the fore-and-aft direction; forestays prevent a mast from collapsing aftward, and backstays prevent a mast from collapsing forward (stays that prevent sideways movement are called shrouds, not stays). Stays take their name from the masts they support; thus, the mainstay supports the mainmast, being secured at or near the base of the next mast forward (i.e., the foremast).

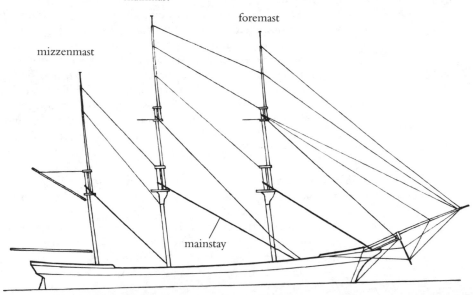

mainmast

foremast

mizzenmast

mainstay

The mainmast is so named because it carries the largest and most important sails. The loss of such a mast, in battle or exceptional weather, often rendered the vessel unmanageable. Such an event was likely if the mast's mainstay (together with perhaps the helper or preventer stay) was shot away; if the wind was then accidentally permitted to get round onto the forward side of the sails, the mast was certain to be brought down, because the wind pressure on the sails would not be counteracted by the forward pull of the mainstay. Colloquially, one's mainstay is a person or object that continually proves to be of great help in one's work or life.

Mainstream
To be in the mainstream

Colloquially, to be the dominant trend, the chief tendency, as in a stage of development; for example, in the realm of fashion. From the nautical use of *stream,* which is a steady current in a river or ocean (such as the Gulf Stream). It is also the main body of water in the tide as it ebbs or flows. A vessel might or might not wish to find itself in the mainstream, according to its port of destination, weather conditions, any local hazards, and so on.

Make
On the make

When a vessel is able to keep to a desired course when tacking, it is said to be "on the make." The phrase is also sailor's slang for feathering one's nest. The everyday colloquialism carries much the same meaning: to be on the lookout for oneself, to look after Number One, to be keen to get ahead.

To make up

An old term from the fisheries; it means to conclude a fishing voyage and settle wage and expense accounts. The ground-sense is that of settlement, and we find this in the common expression *to make up* with somebody, i.e., to become reconciled after a disagreement.

Marine
A dead marine

A marine (from the Latin *marinus,* of the sea) is a seagoing soldier. Marines have been an established and recognised force in the Royal navy since 1755, and were familiarly known—especially to sailors—as "jollies" or "leathernecks." Most naval nations have a marine corps, but in very few cases, except in Britain and the United States, do they actually serve at sea. The marines of both countries have won an enviable reputation for courage, discipline, and fighting skill.

Sailors also used to refer to empty bottles as "marines" because, in their view, both were useless. Legend has it that the Duke of Clarence (York, in another version) was dining in the mess on board one of his ships. When he ordered the steward to remove the "dead marines," one of the officers present protested, to which the Duke replied that, like the marines, the bottle had done its duty nobly and was ready to do so again.

Lind (see bibliography) suggests that the expression originated from the alleged custom in French ships of carrying the bodies of their dead back to port for burial. If the ship was sunk or wrecked on the voyage home, the bodies often floated to the surface. This explanation seems unlikely for two reasons. First, why would the dead bodies of *French* seamen give rise to the expression? The term *marine,* with reference to seagoing soldiers, is British in origin (1664). Second, very few French nautical words and phrases have been adopted by the English; virtually all English seafaring expressions of foreign origin are from the Dutch, Scandinavian, and Germanic languages, in that order.

Empty bottles, especially beer bottles, are today still frequently called "dead marines," and in Australia and England people who are licensed to collect bottles for reuse are called "marine dealers" or "marine collectors." In America an empty liquor bottle is often called a "dead soldier." The

to the fact that in the American armed services, the marines
enjoy a particularly proud and honourable reputation, of
which they are fiercely jealous. It may be that American
sailors (and American marines in particular) are reluctant
to entertain the notion of a dead marine.

To *tell it to the marines* is to express disbelief, to indicate
that the story one has just heard is an extremely unlikely
one; as to say that the marines themselves, notwithstanding
their discipline and obedience, would never believe such a
tale. However, it is equally valid to say that because the
marines have served their country in every part of the
world, and have vast experience, then if they will believe
an otherwise unlikely story, it must be true.

Maul
To be mauled; to maul

"A man that beareth false witness
against his neighbour is a maul,
and a sword, and a sharp arrow."
—Proverbs 25:18

A maul is a heavy wooden or iron hammer used in the
operation of caulking. The caulking iron, a type of wide,
blunt chisel, is driven into the seams between the planks by
the maul, and the oakum in the seam is thereby tightly
secured. Also, *to maul a ship* was to engage it in battle and
rake it repeatedly with broadside after broadside. The ground
sense is to handle roughly, to injure through rough
treatment; the idea of force is present in both usages.

Mayday

Under international radio regulations, *Mayday* is the
radio-telephonic distress signal used by ships or aircraft. It is
primarily a voice signal, as distinct from "SOS" and "CQD,"
which are telegraphic or Morse signals. The phrase is the
English phoneticisation of the French *m'aidez,* help me.

Mayonnaise

A sauce made with pepper, salt, oil, vinegar, egg yolk,
and sometimes other seasonings, beaten up together into
a thick paste. Not a nautical word, but certainly nautical
in origin. When the Duc de Richelieu captured Port
Mahon, Minorja, in 1756, he came ashore and demanded to

be fed. There being no prepared meal, he took whatever he could find and beat it up together; hence the original form *mahonnaise,* which in English became the modern *mayonnaise.*

John Byng, the English admiral in charge of relieving the British garrison that the French had put under siege on Minorca, was court-martialled for failing to do his utmost to recapture the island. He was found guilty and sentenced to death, and finally was shot on the quarterdeck of HMS *Monarch* in 1757. His execution inspired Voltaire's famous remark that in England it was sometimes necessary to shoot an admiral *pour encourager les autres,* "to encourage the others."

Mess
To lose the number of his mess

Seamen in the days of fighting sail had their hammocks numbered in sequential order; this was also their mess number, the number of the group with which each man habitually ate his meals. This was one method of keeping track of a ship's complement and was certainly a convenient way of organising meals, watches, and the like. When a seaman died, his numbered hammock would be unoccupied for a time, and his death meant that he had lost (ceased to have title to) his hammock and mess number.

To mess about; to mess around

"He took and sent messes unto them . . . but Benjamin's mess was five times so much as any of theirs."
—Genesis 43:34

From *mess,* the group of four at a meal; *to be messing with* is to be allocated a mess, an eating area on board ship (from Latin *missum* to Italian *messa,* a course of a meal). In the Inns of Court, London, a mess also consists of four persons.

Seamen of all backgrounds and natures ate together in dimly lit, badly aired spaces below decks, to the accompaniment of shouted conversation, drunken fighting, belching, and farting, which was the generally raucous behaviour to be expected of men who were often the dregs of society and who were, for the most part, treated as such by their officers. Life afloat, particularly aboard a vessel in the older days of the sailing navy, was usually much harder than the hardest life ashore.

To mess about and *to mess around* are colloquialisms meaning to busy oneself in an untidy or confused way; to waste time or to play the fool. American usage favours *to mess around,* which can also carry the additional meaning of being unfaithful in one's sexual responsibilities.

> "There is nothing—absolutely nothing half so much worth doing as simply messing about in boats."
>
> —Kenneth Grahame (1859–1932), British writer, *The Wind in the Willows* (1908)

To mess together; to make a mess of things; to get into a mess

Originally the term *mess* referred to a portion of food; then it came to mean food that had been mixed together; and ultimately a jumble or confusion. A parallel meaning developed that stood for a group of people, usually four, who sat together and ate from the same dishes. Hence the "mess" found in the armed forces, the place where meals are served and eaten *en masse.* Colloquially, the word derives from the crowded and often noisy and confusing nature of the mess, or mess-hall.

For hundreds of years, British seamen messed under what was known as the "standard messing system." In this arrangement, the items of staple diet in the sailor's daily ration, such as meat, potatoes, bread, flour, peas, jam, tea, sugar, and so on (when available) were issued in bulk to each individual mess. The food was then prepared by each mess cook, and taken to the galley for heating and cooking. It wasn't until the twentieth century that "general" messing was introduced and accepted, whereby all meals were cooked by the catering branch in a centralised system of galleys.

Monkey
Freeze the balls of/off a brass monkey

A coarse expression from the days of sail, which now means extremely cold, sufficiently cold to produce the interesting effect alluded to in the expression. In fact, the phrase derives from the brass cannon called a "monkey" in the seventeenth century. In very cold temperatures, the iron cannonballs and the brass cannon would contract at markedly different rates, so much so that the gun would be unusable. Sailors referred to this phenomenon as "freezing the balls of a brass monkey," the key word being *of,* not *off,* and hence the expression was literally true at the time.

Monkey-jacket

A "monkey-jacket" was the short coat worn by seamen, so called because it had no tail or skirt to it (in the same way that a monkey—more strictly, an ape—has no tail). It was also called a "jackanapes coat," from its imagined likeness to the jacket worn by the monkey belonging to the organ grinder of those days. It was generally close-fitting and made of thick material such as serge, and was worn for watch-keeping duties in cold or stormy weather; its shortness kept the legs free for climbing aloft. The closeness of cut and fit led to the modern formal dinner jacket being named after the original naval garment.

Moonlighting

"The prisoners, with two other men, were arrested on a charge of moonlighting [nighttime raids] in county Clare."

—*The Daily Chronicle* (English newspaper), January 17, 1888

The carrying on of activities, especially illegal ones, by moonlight. Originally nautical, referring to smugglers who landed their contraband goods at night. The expression now means that one is holding two jobs, working at the second after finishing one's regular, full-time employment for the day (or night, as the case may be).

N

Nausea

That feeling in the stomach familiar to persons who are susceptible to motion sickness: a sensation of impending vomiting; also a feeling of extreme disgust. From the Greek *nausia,* seasickness. When nausea is combined with a drunken headache, the resulting condition is nicely expressed by the word *crapulous.*

Navy blue

Dark blue, a colour long associated with the Royal Navy; hence its name.

Edward the Confessor (d. 1066) set up a fleet of ships chartered from the barons of the Cinque Ports and crewed by "shipmen" (the then-common term for a seaman, and used by Chaucer in his *Canterbury Tales* in the late fourteenth century), who wore a type of uniform made of coarse woollen cloth dyed blue. This was a form of camouflage, and in fact the Romans a thousand years earlier had used clothing and sails of a similar dark blue colour when they patrolled the coasts of Britain to keep watch for the approach of enemy vessels. In the sixteenth century, British seamen in search of the famed but elusive Northwest Passage wore clothing of "watchet," a sky-coloured material made in the town of Watchet, Somerset.

However, it was many years before blue was adopted as the standard colour for navy dress. Because of the temporary nature of a ship's commission, the men who manned them wore pretty much what they liked. Then, in the early 1600s, the slop system was established. In 1663, the Duke of York detailed the type of clothing seamen had to wear; included were blue shirts and blue neckcloths, all to be drawn by the men from the slops chest against their pay. For many years, red and white cloth also figured in the dress that seamen were beginning to wear in a more or less organised fashion. By the end of the eighteenth century, the predominant colour was blue (jackets, breeches, and waistcoats) and at about this time long trousers began to appear. The term *bluejacket,* the name by which British seamen have long been known, came into being at the beginning of the 1800s, when they adopted a blue jacket as an essential part of their dress.

Early in 1857, the Admiralty recommended that sailors in the British navy wear a "regulated" form of dress: jacket, trousers, frock, peajacket, all of blue serge or "jean," together with hat, tapes, silk handerchief, etc. The "navy blue" uniform was officially adopted by the Admiralty toward the end of that year, and promulgated by appropriate regulations. The term has long since been absorbed into the language as a description of a particular colour.

Nip

"Young Eyre took a full nip of whiskey."
—William Black (1841–1898),
A Princess of Thule (1873)

A small drink, a sip; more specifically, a small (legal) measure of spirits as served in a bar or tavern. From the Dutch *nipperkin,* a small measure, and into the English language via the extensive maritime trade that existed for centuries between England and the Low Countries.

Nipper

Slang for a small boy; still in widespread use in England and Australia. From the fact that when an anchor was heaved-in, the large hemp anchor cable was frequently too heavy to be brought round the capstan. A smaller endless cable, called a "messenger," was passed with a few turns around the capstan and led forward so that it would run close alongside the anchor cable; it thence returned to the capstan.

As the capstan was turned, the anchor cable was quickly temporarily bound to the messenger by short lengths of rope called "nippers." Several nippers were required in this operation, and they were worked by young boys or men who had to be nimble and alert as they bent to their tasks. Colloquially, *nipper* still refers to a small boy who is generally always full of energy and mischief.

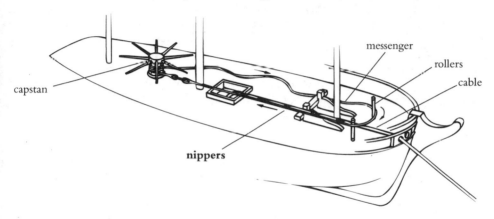

Noggin

A noggin is a small cup or mug; it can also refer to a small quantity of liquor, usually a quarter of a pint. "Nog" was a kind of strong beer brewed in East Anglia. *Noggin* was also the sailor's word for a tub fashioned from a cut-down cask or keg; the origin of the word is obscure. As a slang expression, *noggin* commonly refers to one's head, one's loaf.

Number
I've got your number

You don't fool me; I can see through your game; I twig. The emphasis is upon recognition, and the usage derives from the fact that each merchant vessel from every maritime nation in the world is allocated, by international agreement, a group of four letters that constitutes her recognition signal. This signal is made, when necessary, by hoisting flags in the International Code of Signals, and it is called, oddly enough, the ship's "number."

Clearly, it was—and still is—important for a vessel to be able to correctly identify another vessel on the high seas in time of war; indeed, it was a favourite tactic of certain enemy ships to camouflage their outlines, hoist a false number or recognition signal when challenged, and then to attack the unsuspecting victim. *To have someone's number* under these circumstances would be to see through the deception, and to take whatever action was appropriate.

Your number is up From the days of fighting sail, when ships belonging to a fleet were allotted a number for the purposes of quick and easy signalling during the heat of battle. Often the admiral would call a conference of his captains aboard his flagship, and would signal his intentions by flying the number of the ships whose captains he wished to confer with (in fact, a ship's number was a block of four letters, not digits). As each distinguishing number or identifying code was hoisted on the admiral's ship, so it was said to be "up."

It not infrequently happened that a captain would be summoned for a less-than-cordial conference with the admiral, during which the erring officer might be roundly castigated by his superior officer for some lapse in conduct. Hence, when a captain saw his ship's number flown by the admiral as a recall signal, he could never be certain of his reception on board the flagship.

The colloquial usage means "You are caught," "All is up with you," "You are in serious trouble." It also carries the additional meaning of "You are about to die"; usually expressed by the seaman as "to lose the number of his mess

Oars
To put / shove / stick in one's oar

To interrupt, to interfere, to break into a conversation to say one's piece; to add one's bit; as when one applies one's oar to help pull a boat through the water. From an older expression, "to have an oar in another man's boat," meaning to have an interest in someone else's affairs. The widespread use of this once purely nautical term is a measure of how thoroughly maritime terminology has permeated everyday speech.

To rest on one's oars

The oar is one of the best-known adjuncts of life at sea. It is, in its oldest form, a wooden pole flattened at one end, which, when used as a lever, pulls a boat through the water. It has three parts: the blade, the shaft, and the loom (the inboard end on which the rower pulls).

Rowing—pulling on the oars—is a very strenuous activity; colloquially, then, to rest on one's oars is to take a spell, a breather, after a period of hard work or intense physical effort. The original phrase was "to lie upon one's oars."

Off and on

Also "on and off." Colloquially, this phrase has the force of "now and then," or "sometimes it is, sometimes it isn't," "occasionally": "I see him off and on at the club." Originally it referred to a vessel's deliberate tactic of alternately sailing toward the land (on) and then away from it (off). This was done (most often at night) when she was waiting for her pilot, or when entering an unfamiliar harbour. The emphasis was upon the deliberate back-and-forth movement of the vessel.

Offing
In the offing

"The discrepancy in the estimate of the vessel's offing. . . ."

—*The Daily News* (English newspaper), September 30, 1881

The offing is that vaguely defined part of the sea lying between the horizon and the harbour entrance or coastal waters; it is the expanse of ocean that can be seen from any particular point on shore. To *keep an offing* is to keep a distance away from land because of navigational hazards, bad weather, or the like; to keep clear of all danger. Ships visible at sea from land are said to be "in the offing," that is, they are often about to approach port or some nearby anchorage. The term has come to mean "about to happen"; if a storm, wedding, election, or other event is likely to occur, then it is said to be "in the offing."

Oil
To pour oil on troubled waters

To soothe ruffled tempers; to use tact and gentle words to restore peace after an argument: "He is always getting into strife with people, and his wife spends a lot of time pouring oil on troubled waters." From the well-known fact that oil floats on water, and that when poured onto the surface of a stormy sea it very markedly decreases the violence of the waves. In a storm, the usual method was to hang an oil bag over the side of the vessel and allow the oil to drip into the sea. An oil slick would form, thus preventing the waves from breaking.

Oldster

"Leave all us oldsters to bore one another to death."

—Henry Kingsley (1830–1876), English novelist, *Ravenshoe* (1862)

An old navy term, from the days of fighting sail, for a midshipman who had more than four years' seniority to his credit. He occupied the cockpit of the ship with the master's mates, who were also known as "oldsters." Junior midshipmen of less than four years' seniority messed in the gunroom, under the supervision of the gunner. The term is well-known in colloquial speech; it refers to an older person.

Overbear

Originally a nautical term to describe a wind that overwhelms a ship. *To overbear* is to bear over or bear down by weight or force; to overcome; to domineer.

Overbearing

To be domineering or dictatorial; arrogant or haughty, generally rude. From a combination of *to bear up* (to bring a vessel even closer to the wind) and *to bear down upon* (to approach another vessel from the windward side and thus be in a position of great advantage). The common element is one that suggests intimidation.

Overboard
To go overboard about something

"All of us sacrifice our sins, cast them overboard. . . ."
—Brinsley, *A Groan for Israel,* cited in the *Universal Dictionary of the English Language* (1897)

Board is from the Old English *bord,* meaning board, plank, table. *To board* meant to enter a ship by force; *aboard* describes the state of being in—never "on"—a ship. *To go overboard* meant that something had fallen over the side; in the case of a member of the crew going over the side, the cry is "Man overboard!" When a mast or some other substantial piece of gear was carried away by storm or battle, it was said *to go by the board, board* being the general term for the ship's deck.

Used figuratively, the phrase means to harbour an excess of feeling about something, to lose one's emotional footing, as it were, and plunge into a wave of unbridled enthusiasm.

Overhaul

"The 20-ton cutter *Irene* is getting a complete overhaul."
—*Field Magazine,* April 4, 1885

The phrase nowadays means to inspect, test, and repair machinery or the like, but originally it meant to increase the distance between two sets of blocks in a tackle system, by running the rope back through the sheaves; i.e., to separate the two sets of blocks still further. To bring them so close together as to prevent further relative movement between the blocks is to cause them to be "block and block." *To overhaul* also means to gain steadily upon some other vessel, vehicle, runner, or such, so as eventually to pass it.

Over-rated

"Overrate their happiness...."
—Thomas Babington Macaulay
(1800–1859), English historian,
History of England (1848)

The rank held by a naval seaman is known as a "rate," and the man himself as a "rating" (one who fills that rate or position). Each seaman held a rate according to his ability. If he entered the ship as a boy, he became an ordinary seaman (the first rating) at age 18, and—other things being equal—he was rated an "able-bodied" seaman (an "A.B.," which properly means one who could "hand, reef, and steer") at about age 21.

From there he could be promoted successively to Leading Seaman, Petty Officer (from the French *petit,* small), and so on. In the early days of sail—for example, in the Royal Navy at the time of the French Revolutionary Wars and the Napoleonic Wars (1792–1814)—the avenues of promotion were a little more flexibly organised, but at the same time a seaman had fewer promotional positions for which he could strive.

Captains could rate their own men; indeed, they had to after any battle that took its usually high toll of casualties. It often happened that, in the nature of things, a man was rated to a position for which he was unsuitable either by skill or temperament or both. In time he would be found to be "over-rated," in which case the captain could, if he wished, derate the seaman to a lower rating. Derating was also a common means of punishment, as a disciplinary measure against, for example, frequent drunkenness or insolence to an officer. In a similar fashion, a man might be found to be "under-rated," deserving of promotion to a rate that he was better fitted for.

Hence the metaphors that have been derived from this nautical practice: *to be over-rated* is to be overestimated, overvalued; and *to be under-rated* is the reverse, to be held at too low a value.

Overwhelm

Nautically, to be buried by an onrushing and breaking sea, as in broaching; to be unable to resist the combined forces of

"Humming water must
o'erwhelm thy corpse. . . ."
—William Shakespeare (1564–1616),
Pericles, act 3, scene 1

the prevailing weather conditions. As a figure of speech, the phrase means to be overcome completely in mind or feeling; to be defeated by force of numbers.

Over is from the Old English *ofer,* which in turn derives from the Sanskrit *upari,* above in place or position. *Whelm,* which itself is the archaic word for to submerge, to engulf ("sorrow whelmed her"), is a combining of the Old English *gehwelfan,* bend over, and *helmian,* cover.

P

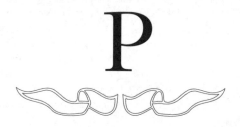

Parcel *To parcel* is to wrap fabric, such as hessian or canvas, around the end of a rope that has been "wormed"—prepared for parcelling—to ready it for serving, so that the rope end will be protected from the rot that constant wetting will otherwise induce. Usually the fabric used for parcelling was tarred canvas. *To worm* a rope is to lay a thin line in the grooves or lays of the larger rope; *to serve* (originally, "sarve") is to wind spun yarn tightly and closely over the parcelling, so that the completed work is firmly bound together and is virtually waterproof. The old rule for this complete operation is: "Worm and parcel with the lay, Turn and serve the other way." The word *parcel* was certainly in use some 300 years before the parcel post was established in England in 1883, but it is not clear whether the nautical usage preceded general usage.

Pass To be accepted as or recognised as what one purports to be.
To pass for The phrase is from the old naval form; when a midshipman had served the requisite number of years afloat (generally, six years), he took an examination for the rank of lieutenant. If he was successful, he was said "to pass for" lieutenant. The phrase is peculiarly nautical: in all other fields of endeavour and examination we "pass the test" rather than pass "for" the objective.

Pay
To pay off

Originally, *to pay off* was to close the accounts of a naval ship when she reached the end of a commission; all the ship's company were then given the balance of monies due to them. Merchant seamen were paid off at the end of a voyage. Many a naval vessel in the seventeenth century was sent straight back to sea after having come in to port to be paid off, for want of cash on the part of the Navy Board. It was not uncommon for seamen—and thus their wives and families—to be denied their regular wages for years on end. How seamen's dependents lived ashore under these conditions, in the hard times of that century, defies the imagination.

In the colloquial sense, *to pay someone off* is to get even, to exact retribution, to pay off an old score; from the earlier sense of closing the accounts: "The foreman had been unnecessarily harsh with us on the assembly line, but we paid him off by sabotaging the production machinery." Rendered also by the expression *to pay someone out*— i.e., "I'll be a match for him, I'll get even."

Peepers

Sailor's slang for eyes; the expression was in common use in ships at the beginning of the 1800s. The word has long since passed into common use, and is enshrined in at least one 1938 song of music-hall fame, the first line of which runs: "Jeepers Creepers, where'd you get those peepers?"

Peg
To take one down a peg

"The brilliant young athlete wanted taking down a peg."

—*Literary World*, February 3, 1882, cited in the *Universal Dictionary of the English Language* (1897)

To deflate a conceited person; to puncture his pretension, to damage his self-esteem. From the manner in which signals and flags (the ship's colours) were attached to the halyard by which they were hoisted. They were secured to the halyard by toggles, a simple peg-and-loop arrangement similar to the fastenings on duffel coats. The higher a ship's colours were raised, the greater the honour, and to cause them to be taken down a peg would be to diminish the honour.

Pickled To be very drunk. One contemporary authority (Lind; see bibliography) suggests that this expression refers particularly to the pickling of Lord Nelson's body in a cask of brandy for transit back to England after the Battle of Trafalgar in 1805. This origin may be correct, but it seems just as likely that, by popular analogy, the consumption of large quantities of alcohol would also pickle one from the inside, so to speak.

However, the manner of returning Nelson's body to England did give rise to a widespread (albeit erroneous) belief among British seamen not only that rum was used for the task, but also that the sentries tapped (siphoned off) some of this rum while they were guarding the cask. Both stories are, of course, untrue: brandy, not rum, was used, and the cask was so charged with the gasses of putrefaction from the body's organs that the head of the cask began to lift, causing great alarm to the sentries and necessitating the replenishment of the brandy a number of times. It is highly unlikely that any seaman or soldier would have broached Nelson's coffin-cask in these circumstances.

It has also been suggested that the expression *drunk as a lord* owes its origin to the same set of incidents. This, too, seems unlikely, although it is obvious why seamen would have regarded Nelson as being thoroughly drunk, steeped in brandy as he was. The expression would certainly have been in common usage before Nelson's time; excessive drinking was common among the nobility of the eighteenth and nineteenth centuries, and many a man of fashion and title prided himself on the number of bottles of wine he could consume at a sitting.

Pile up Nautically, to run a vessel ashore or aground on a shoal or rock; colloquially, to crash, to come to grief.

Pillage

First used as a noun (fourteenth century); from the French *piller,* to plunder, and earlier from the Low Latin *piliare,* to pill (obsolete for "to peel").

By ancient law of the sea, the captors of a ship had the right to seize any goods that were strewn on the upper deck; what often happened was that the holds were broken open and their contents scattered on the deck, to be immediately picked up a moment later and claimed as pillage. Nowadays the term means to strip of money or goods by open violence, on land as well as on sea; to take as booty; to rob and plunder.

Pinch
At a pinch; in a pinch

To pinch-up is to sail a vessel so close to the wind that her sails shiver and consequently her speed is reduced. Sometimes it is possible to just fetch, or round, a desired mark by deliberately pinching the vessel up to the wind, even though considerable way may be lost. Similarly, when something can be done "at a pinch," a sacrifice—or a threat of a sacrifice—of some kind may be necessary; one may then just scrape through.

Pipe
To pipe down

From the call made by the boatswain (bosun) on a naval vessel, generally made last thing at night. The call is done with the bosun's pipe or whistle, and is the order for lights out and all hands to turn in (to go to their bunks); for silence generally. The phrase is in wide use, meaning to verbally restrain someone from being too noisy or aggressive, or making a nuisance of herself: "Will you pipe down for a minute? I want to listen to the news." From the Anglo-Saxon *pipe* and the Latin *pipare,* to pipe or cheep, like a young bird.

To pipe up

Probably formed in the language as the antithesis of *to pipe down.* Its origin is likely not nautical, because *to pipe up* means to call—on the bosun's pipe—the watch from below to their duties on deck. As the off-duty watch is nearly always turned in and asleep, a bosun's pipe would be unlikely to be heard. Instead, the bosun's mates invariably called the seamen in person.

The expression means to begin to talk, especially unexpectedly; to make oneself heard; to speak up and assert oneself. All these senses are opposite to those of "pipe down." The expression is used nautically, though, to describe a wind that is beginning to pick up, to increase noticeably in strength.

Piping hot

Food that is hot, freshly cooked, straight from the ovens; a familiar domestic expression. It originates from the days when seamen were piped to their meals with the bosun's pipe or call; when the men heard the mess-call on the pipe, they knew that the food was hot and ready for serving.

Piss
Poor as piss and twice as nasty

Sailor's slang for anything that is really bad; the expression needs little by way of explanation. *Piss* is from the French *pisser,* from the Latin *pissare,* probably imitative in origin of the act of urinating. It is interesting that the Teutonic languages borrowed the word originally as a euphemism.

The expression has found great favour among the cognoscenti of the various brands of beer available in Australia. For those whose interest is now aroused, *pisco* was a potent liquor brewed in Peru and on the Chilean coast (from a Spanish word, which in turn is also from the Latin source *pissare)*. The name was shortened in English to "pis" or "piss," and applied to any cheap drink of dubious origin and quality.

Pitch
To pitch and pay

To pay up at once; from the fact that vessels had their seams sealed with pitch, that is, "payed." The task could be done properly only when the pitch to be applied was hot. The original sense of *pay*—to pour hot pitch into a seam caulked with oakum—was not connected with *pay* in the sense of money or debt. The one became linked with the other because of the idea of immediacy or requirement necessarily attached to both.

Pitch in

To deal with something, to sort some matter out, to encourage others to help in a common cause. From the notion of cooperation required when seamen were paying pitch into the seams of a vessel.

Plot
To plot a course of action

"Here's the plot on't. . . ."
—Ben Jonson (1572–1637), English dramatist and poet, *The Alchemist* (1610)

From the Anglo-Saxon *plot,* patch of ground. The word gradually developed a number of meanings, all deriving from the basic idea of an area or patch of earth, and thence to plan and design. Thus, "to plot a course" is to mark on a chart the intended direction of the vessel; to determine such a course. By extension, the figurative usage is clear: to plan a course of action that will lead toward some desired objective.

Plug

Originally a nautical word from the Dutch and found in the German *pflock,* a peg or plug, as in a bung or stopper. The stopper fitted in the bottom of a ship's boat, which enables it to be drained when hoisted aboard or onto the beach, is called the "plug." A "plug" of tobacco is named for its plug-like shape. *To plug on*—to work hard—is from rowing.

Ply
To ply back and forth

"We plyed all the floods to the windewardes."
—Richard Hakluyt (?1552–1616), English cleric and maritime historian, *Principall Navigations, Voiages, and Discoveries of the English Nation* (1589)

Descriptive of a vessel as it makes regular voyages between certain ports, often scheduled, but not always; to ply for trade; to seek cargoes by sailing or steaming from one port to another as opportunity offers, as did tramp steamers earlier in this century. The word is a variation of the Middle English *aplye,* to apply. The word found its first application in this sense by seamen, in particular the Thames watermen. It is now used generally to mean to carry on, to practise, to pursue.

"The word is Pitch and pay: Trust none."
—William Shakespeare (1564–1616), *Henry V,* act 2, scene 3

Point blank

"Point-blank over against the mouth of the piece."

—Brewer, *Lingua,* cited in the *Universal Dictionary of the English Language* (1897)

From the French *point blanc,* white point or centre, the white disk that marks the bull's-eye of a target. When a ship's gun is fired "point blank," it is fired at a distance (usually quite short) such that if the line of sight to the target is parallel with the axis of the barrel (i.e., as if one were sighting at the enemy target by peering down the bore of the barrel instead of along it), then the projectile will travel direct, without curve or deviation, to hit the object at the point of aim. At point blank range, the gun is close enough to hit the bull's-eye without having to allow for the curve of trajectory.

Hence the colloquialism: to be direct, to the point, without beating about the bush; straightforward.

Poles
Under bare poles

To be *under bare poles* means to have no sails set, because of bad weather. The vessel invariably still makes headway, being driven by the force of the wind on the masts and spars. Figuratively, the phrase applies to a person who is driven to his last extremity; to be broke, down on one's luck.

Poop
To be pooped

"A press of canvas that may have saved her from being pooped."

—*The Daily Telegraph* (English newspaper), November 12, 1885

The poop deck is the highest deck at the stern of a sailing vessel, raised (where fitted) above the quarterdeck. From the Latin *puppis,* stern. A ship is "pooped" when a heavy sea breaks over her stern while she is running before the wind in a gale—a very dangerous situation, because the vessel's speed in this circumstance is approximately the same as that of the following sea. She therefore loses steerage way and becomes uncontrollable, with the likelihood of broaching-to and foundering. *To be pooped* metaphorically is to be exhausted, finished, at one's last resort.

Posh

There are two explanations for the origin of this word, which means stylish, high-class, upper-class, as in "a posh hotel," "posh clothes," "a posh accent."

The most commonly accepted story is that it comes from the heyday of the British Empire, when travel from Britain to India, Australia, and the Far East was by P&O steamship through the Suez Canal (the Peninsula and Oriental Steam Navigation Company carried mails and passengers between England and India in the period 1842–1970).

The passage down the Red Sea and across the Indian Ocean north of the equator was, at the best of times, an unbearably hot one. It is said that passengers booking the return journey from Britain to the colonies would try to secure a cabin for the outward-bound journey on the port side of the vessel—i.e., on the left-hand side. Because the ship was approaching the equator from the north and west, the sun was always on the right-hand or starboard side in the afternoon, the hottest part of the day. Choosing a cabin on the port side would put the passenger on the side of the ship that was presumably a little cooler in the evening. Similarly, the voyage home would be booked for the starboard side, as this part of the vessel would be away from the direct glare of the afternoon sun.

This story insists that the P&O booking clerk would endorse the ticket "POSH," their acronym for "Port Out, Starboard Home." Naturally, because of the demand for these better-located berths, the steamship company would charge a premium on the fare. Consequently, the acronym POSH became associated with travellers who could afford the higher fare, and they themselves became known as "posh," people who belonged to a better or higher class.

However, there is one major obstacle to this story, despite its widespread acceptance—there appears to be no evidence to support it. Officials of the P&O Steamship Company have asserted that there is no record at all of tickets ever being endorsed in the manner just detailed.

In 1937, Mr. Boyd Cable published *A Hundred Year History of the P&O,* in which he described the story behind "posh" as

"He has not got the posh [money] yet."

—*Sessions Paper Old Bailey* (1824–1833), cited in the *Oxford English Dictionary Supplement* (1982)

"Practically every posh family in the country has called him in at one time or another."

—P. G. Wodehouse (1881–1975), *The Inimitable Jeeves* (1924)

a "tale"; and in 1962 the librarian of the P&O reported that he could find no evidence that the initials POSH were ever stamped on the company's tickets or documents of any kind.

Indeed, one must ask the obvious question: Why would a P&O booking clerk need to stamp a ticket in any particular way at all? The clerks would be perfectly familiar with the arrangement of the cabins on the company's ships, and if a passenger wanted a berth on the cooler port side on the voyage to India, it would have been a simple matter for the booking clerk to give him or her the appropriately numbered ticket. It may well be, of course, that people who were familiar with travel in this region might have themselves devised the POSH acronym as a means of passing on advice to others making the trip for the first time, but it is certainly not the case that the P&O Company used it in their booking arrangements.

The second (and less colourful) story is the more likely of the two. The word almost certainly derives from the Romany slang word *posh,* meaning both "dandy" and "money." *(Romany* is the name preferred by so-called gypsy peoples.) In this slang, anyone who had a bit of money was a "dandy," a "swell," or what in America would be called a "swank" person, and who was therefore said to be "posh." In time, *posh* came to be associated with the comfort and convenience that money could buy, as well as with anyone who was stylish or who affected high-class manners.

Posh, to mean stylish, swank, is no longer as current as it used to be, although it is still understood in the English-speaking world. It enjoyed a heyday at the turn of the century, and was to be found in the novels of P. G. Wodehouse, the British writer. Today it would be used as a description of a person or a place.

Post
To be posted

In the Royal Navy there were two grades of captain. Lieutenants who were promoted to captain were given the command of a small ship other than a rated vessel; after sufficient experience in command of such a ship, they were then "posted" (given command of) a rated ship, where they took the rank of post-captain.

The phrase is commonly used nowadays as in *to be posted* to the country, interstate, overseas, etc., or to be given a post in a firm. It is also found in expressions such as "trading post" and the "last post" (a military bugle call).

The word is from the Italian *posto* and the Latin *positus,* placed, put.

Press

From the Latin *pressare,* to press, and *praestare,* to warrant, vouch for, to perform. Not to be confused with the term *prest,* from the Old French *preter,* to land.

To press on

To push on or carry on with all speed, vigor, and power, so as to get the task completed; not to be delayed or waylaid by trifles. The phrase is from the sailor's habit of crowding on as much canvas as conditions would allow to complete the passage as swiftly as possible. Such a vessel might occasionally be "hard pressed," and in any case, if she is setting as much canvas as possible, she is said to be under a "press of sail." From the fact that the square-rigged ship was at her best when sailing before the wind.

Pressed
To be hard-pressed

To be closely pursued, in both the literal and metaphorical senses. "The businessman was hard-pressed by his creditors." The land usage follows the sailor's phrase for describing a ship under a press of canvas; that is, when all working sails are set and are drawing well. The colloquial allusion is to the constant and sometimes overpowering pressure exerted by one's pursuers.

Prime To fill up, as in "to prime the ship's pump." From the Anglo-Saxon *prim* and the Latin *prima*. The earliest sense of the word referred to the loading of a ship; hence the nautical word *primage,* which is a percentage addition to freight charges. A "prime seaman" is one who is fully trained and experienced; one who can hand, reef, and steer. The "prime meridian" is longitude 0°, and is now internationally agreed to be the meridian of longitude that passes through Greenwich, England. It is from Greenwich that longitudes are measured east or west. *To prime,* in ordinary usage, is to prepare or make ready for a particular purpose.

Proof spirit The system of labelling spiritous liquors today as over-proof or under-proof derives from the early method of treating Jamaica rum in the navy victualling yards before issuing it to naval ships.

The rum arrived in England at 140 degrees over-proof; it was then reduced to 95.5 degrees under-proof by having water added to it in certain proportions. This was done by pouring a small amount of the alcohol-and-water mixture over some grains of gunpowder and igniting it, usually with a magnifying glass. If the burning alcohol then just managed to ignite the gunpowder, the mixture was said to be "proof"; if it exploded, it was "over-proof"; and if the gunpowder failed to ignite at all it was, of course, "under-proof." Proof spirit today is legally defined as that which has a specific gravity of 12/13 (92.3 percent) at 51°F.

Pull
To pull together *To pull,* in most navies, is to row a boat with oars. Naval tradition defines the activity as "pulling," not "rowing." The oars are pivoted in small yokes called "rowlocks" (pronounced "roll-ocks"). If the pulling boat is to be moved from one place to another smartly and efficiently (as in transferring the captain to shore, or abandoning a

vessel that has a fire near its powder magazine), then the **129**
seamen must pull together, in time and with a will.

Similarly, in a figurative sense, people who have a common
goal must work together and cooperate as a team, as in a
sports match or other endeavour.

Put
To put in for
A vessel is said "to put in for" a particular harbour or port
when she enters it, or intends to enter it; especially when
turning aside from her regular course to seek shelter, repairs,
provisions, and the like. Colloquially, the expression means
to make application, to make a bid, as in applying for a
position.

Quarter
To blow from another quarter

When the wind shifts, it is said to blow from another quarter. As a metaphor, the expression describes the situation when a person being argued with is attacked—verbally—by another person or from a different point of view.

Quarters

From the French *quartier* and the Latin *quartarius,* fourth part, a measure.

The word has very early specialised nautical applications. Sailors speak of the wind as blowing from a particular quarter. The quarterdeck is that part of the upper deck of a ship aft of the mainmast. In medieval British warships, the religious shrine was set up on the quarterdeck, and was saluted by every man's taking off his hat or cap as he passed it; British warships still maintain the tradition of saluting the quarterdeck when entering it.

The quartermaster was a petty officer of the fifteenth century, who assisted in maintaining the ship's working gear but who now is associated with steering duties and upkeep of the navigational equipment. The quarterbill is a list of officers and men in a warship showing the action station for every man on board when the ship went into battle. When this happened, the order "Beat to quarters" was given and the ship's drummers would beat out a particular rhythm.

"His praise, ye winds! that from four quarters blow, Breathe soft or loud."
—John Milton (1608–1674), English poet, *Paradise Lost* (1667)

R

Rack and ruin *Rack* here is a variant spelling of "wrack," which is itself another version of "wreck"; but *wrack* and *wreck* have now become differentiated in sense. *Wreck* is from the Anglo-Saxon *wraec,* exile, misery; whereas *wrack* is from the Middle English *wrac,* originally seaweed. *Wrack* later came to mean anything driven ashore by the waves. *Rack and ruin* is a direct outgrowth of *wrack;* as a colloquialism, it means destruction, wreckage, disrepair, collapse (especially that brought about by neglect).

Rake To cause to be slanted or angled; usually the inclination forward or aft from the perpendicular. Also describes the extent to which the stem and stern angle away from the ends of the keel. The early schooners that came out of Gloucester, Massachusetts, were noted for the aft rake of their masts. The word is now used to describe the inclination or slope of a wide range of everyday objects, particularly when that inclination is adjustable; as in the rake of a roof-beam, derrick, cutting face of a machine tool, and so on. From the Swedish *raka,* to project.

Rate
How does it rate? This phrase and its variations derive from the way in which fighting ships took precedence when getting into the line of battle. The colloquialism today emphasises quality (or lack

"I am a spirit
of no common rate."
—William Shakespeare (1564–1616), *A
Midsummer Night's Dream,* act 3, scene 1

thereof): "How does our team rate against the visitors from the city?"

Originally, the phrases that denoted the rating of warships referred solely to the size and number of their armament, not to their efficiency or quality. Seamen in the British and Australian navies are known generally as "ratings."

To be first-rate

When something is said to be "first-rate," it is being held up as a paradigm or model of its class; it is the best available. The phrase derives from the fact that the fighting sail of the Royal Navy were classified into "rates" according to the number of guns carried on board. Thus, a ship with 100 or more guns was a first-rate warship; a second-rater carried between 82 and 100 guns; and so on down to a sixth-rate vessel.

In 1677, Samuel Pepys, as First Secretary to the Admiralty, drew up a manning list that established the number of men to be borne according to a ship's rating (i.e., according to the number of guns she carried). This establishment is shown in the following list (figures taken from Lloyd [see bibliography]):

First Rate: 100 guns/800 men
Second Rate: 82 guns/530 men
Third Rate: 74 guns/460 men
Fourth Rate: 54 guns/280 men
Fifth Rate: 30 guns/130 men
Sixth Rate: fewer than 30 guns/65 men

One notes immediately the enormous number of men carried on the larger vessels; it probably goes a long way toward accounting for the fact that disease was the cause of 50 percent of the navy's casualties during the French and Napoleonic Wars around the turn of the eighteenth century. About one-third of all fatalities were caused by accidents (parting rigging, breaking spars, falling from aloft, drowning, bursting guns, heavy objects such as guns running loose on deck in a gale, uncontrolled anchor cables, and so on); founderings, wrecks, fires, and explosions carried off another 10 percent; and the remainder—less than 10 percent— were those men killed in action, directly or as a result of their wounds. These figures would approximately hold for almost any period of the era of fighting sail; indeed, it is likely that the deaths from disease were much higher in times preceding the end of the eighteenth century, when medical science was (albeit very slowly) beginning to come to grips with the scourges of scurvy, yellow fever, typhus, and smallpox.

"I praised her as I rated her."
—William Shakespeare (1564–1616),
Cymbeline, act 1, scene 4

Pepys's six classifications constituted the ships-of-the-line-of-battle, so named because of the fact that, traditionally, sailing warships entered battle in the formation known as "in line astern," or one behind the other, with the first-rate ships leading the way. Our modern battleships derive their name directly from this nomenclature, sometimes written as "line-of-battle ships."

The colloquial use of "second-rate," "third-rate," and so on follows the analogy of being inferior to the leading or first-rate ships, when entering battle in line astern. "He's not much at pitching, but he's a first-rate batter."

Similarly, seamen were rated according to their ability and experience (Ordinary Seaman, Able Seaman, Leading Seaman, and so on through to the petty officers).

Rattle	*To rattle* someone is to disconcert, to confuse; the phrase *to be in the rattle* is sailor's slang for being in trouble with officialdom, to be run in. The "rattle" is early sailor's slang meaning to be held in irons, to be in the brig (shipboard prison). The term probably comes from the fact that being held in irons occasioned a good deal of noise whenever one moved; hence *rattle.*

Reckoning
Dead reckoning

To calculate a ship's position by plotting on the chart the distance run since the last reliable navigational fix, taking into account speed, tide, current, wind, and any other factors that might have influenced forward motion through the water.

The phrase is said to have evolved from the term *ded. reckoning*, i.e., "deduced reckoning"; another suggestion is that it arose from the seaman's use of the term *dead sea,* to describe the seas shown on some maps hundreds of years ago about which little or nothing was known. For the mariner of that era, any voyage across such a sea would presumably be governed by "dead" reckoning.

In modern times, the term has both its nautical navigational meaning and a similar construction applied to an activity involving sequential steps of some kind, wherein an estimate of one's progress or performance must be made from time to time.

> "It were a pity you should get your living by reckoning, sir."
> —William Shakespeare (1564–1616), *Love's Labour's Lost,* act 5, scene 2

Reel
To reel off

From the reel that held the ship's log line; used in measuring the ship's speed through the water. This reel was held aloft by a seaman or midshipman, the log (properly, the "log-chip" or "chip-log") was heaved astern, and the 28-second sandglass was set running. As the log line was drawn astern by the action of the water on the chip-log, the ship was said to "reel off" her knots, particularly if she was making good speed.

Figuratively, the expression means to say, write, or produce in easy and continuous way, more or less without hesitation: "Without pausing, he began to reel off the previous week's figures for fluctuations in the price of gold." From the Anglo-Saxon *hreol,* reel, and derived from the Old Norse *hraell,* reel.

Robin
Round robin

A petition or protest written in circular form so that no particular signature heads the list, and therefore no one

"The members of the Royal Commission sent to Sir George Grey a sort of round robin."

—*The Daily Telegraph* (English newspaper), February 24, 1886

person can be singled out as a ringleader. From a French custom, probably from *rond ruban,* round ribbon, which was originally used by sailors when urging a formal protest or claim on their superior officers. The urger or instigator of the protest or petition was, of course, known to the others (but not to the authorities), and as a result of the shape of this "round robin" he was known as the "ringleader." Now commonly used to refer to a sporting competition in which each team plays every other team.

Rope
Money for old rope

Something for nothing. Old rope was useless to the sailor (other than for the making of oakum, used in caulking the seams of a wooden vessel), so it was sold to dealers who used it in the paper and book-binding trades. A variation of this expression has "money for jam"—probably of military origin.

Ropes
To know the ropes; to learn the ropes

To acquire the skills and knowledge relating to an occupation; to gradually absorb the details and information that will allow one to function efficiently in one's new environment, as in an apprenticeship or a change in job: "She'll make a very good section-manager once she gets to know the ropes."

The reference is to the fact that sailors had to learn—and quickly—the location and operation of every rope on board ship. They had to be equally proficient at handling the multitude of lifts, braces, tacks, sheets, guys, pendants, halliards, etc., that festooned the vessel, in good weather and bad and in the dark of night as well as in the daylight watches.

Most vessels of similar rig standardised their rigging layout, so that a seaman would be able to carry out his duties quickly and efficiently even if he were to find himself in another vessel. Shipboard apprentices were taught the ropes and tested on their knowledge of them, but a mistake often meant a taste of the rope's end for the lazy or forgetful tyro.

It is worth noting that a large sailing vessel has perhaps only a dozen or so ropes that are so called; some such are "bolt ropes," "foot ropes," "bell ropes," "bucket ropes," "man ropes," "yard ropes," "back ropes," and "top ropes." Otherwise, when a rope is put to use on a vessel, it becomes a "line" (such as a "clew-line") or acquires a particular name (such as "halliard" and "tack").

Round
To round down; to round up; to round to

In general, *to round down* means to gather in the slack of any rope that passes through blocks; to close the space between these blocks when there is no weight on the tackle. *To round down a tackle* is to overhaul it. *To round to* is to bring a sailing vessel up to the wind. Nowadays, the phrase *to round to* is usually rendered as *to round up,* so that a sailing vessel that is rounding up is one that is coming head to wind, with the object either of going off onto the other tack, or of losing sufficient way to come to anchor.

As a metaphor, *to round (up) on someone* is to turn on them, to stop them in their tracks, to bring them to a halt in their explanation or argument: "She rounded on him as soon as he walked through the door, demanding to know why he had not telephoned earlier."

The sailor's equivalent colloquialism is *to be brought up all standing,* more commonly rendered as *to be taken aback.*

Rouse
To rouse in; to rouse out; to rouse up

To rouse out is the old sailing term for turning out the hands for duty or for a muster call. In rope handling, *to rouse* means to pull together; for instance, on an anchor cable or halyard, without the assistance of any mechanical aid such as a capstan.

Widely used in Australia as a colloquialism for organising, stirring up, getting things going; as in "to rouse up a meal," rouse someone from sleep or inactivity, to stir to anger, and so on. "She roused the children away from the TV set and out into the garden."

The word *rouseabout* derives from *rouse,* and describes the general handyman to be found on many Australian sheep and cattle stations, in hotels, and such. It is also a common name for wharf labourers in the United States, but the American form is *roustabout.* The origin of the word *rouse* is obscure, but it may derive from an Old French word *rouse* connected with hunting, with a reference to a hawk ruffling its feathers.

Rummage

This very old nautical term has found a secure place as a colloquialism in our everyday language; its maritime origin is quite unsuspected. It stems from the French *arrumage,* from *arrumer,* to stow goods in a ship's hold. Early meanings also included the moving of cargo for any reason, such as getting at a leak in the hold, or the discarding of ballast and refuse and putting in new ballast.

In modern usage, *to rummage* means to search thoroughly and actively through a place or receptacle of some kind—especially a drawer, cupboard, or the like—for some necessary item: "She began frantically to rummage through her handbag in search of her train ticket." A "rummage sale" is generally a sale of no-longer-needed clothing and other household chattels, often for the purpose of raising funds for charity; but originally a rummage sale was an auction, on the dockside, of unclaimed goods from ships' cargoes.

Run
To cut and run

To escape, to quit in a hurry; to drop whatever one was doing and to leave immediately. The *cut* is in reference to the need for a ship to cut its anchor cable (in the days of sail, a very heavy hempen rope) when danger threatened and it was necessary for the ship to leave its anchorage in the emergency.

Weighing the anchor and stowing the cable below was normally a long and tedious business. When the Spanish Armada was anchored off Calais, most of the captains cut their cables and ran out to sea in an attempt to escape when Howard, the English commander-in-chief, sent his fireships among them.

Originally, the expression derives from the practice of square-rigged ships (when at anchor in an open roadstead), furling their sails by stropping or tying them to the yards with light line instead of the heavier rope used for gaskets. When the need to get underway was urgent, as because of threatening weather or an approaching enemy, the sails could be quickly set by sending men aloft to cut the light rope-yarns. The sails would immediately hang free from their yards in readiness for instant departure. The anchor cable would, of course, either have to be cut, as previously described, with the anchor buoyed for possible future recovery, or the moorings slipped if the vessel happened not to be riding to an anchor.

S

Sailing
It's all plain sailing

Another example of how landsmen have, over the years, innocently corrupted the language of sailors. The expression refers to anything that is straightforward and easy to do; there need be no hesitation about the course of action to be followed.

The expression in fact derives from the earlier phrase *plane sailing,* which is the art of determining a vessel's position on the assumption that the earth is flat and that she is therefore sailing on a plane surface.

For more than a century after the Mercator chart was introduced in 1569, shipmasters were still using plane charts for their navigation, even though the sphericity of the earth made for problems in drafting the meridians onto paper. The use of these plane charts was known as "plane sailing," often written as "plain sailing" because of the ease (i.e., the plainness) with which navigators could use the old established method.

Salt
An old salt

A long-experienced sailor, one who has been at sea a considerable time; often called a "shellback" from the limpets and barnacles that are said to have had time to grow on his back because of his long service at sea. By extension, an "old salt" in any job is someone who has accumulated vast experience and knowledge, and who has much of value to pass on.

Scant

"They [winds] rose or scantled,
as his sails would drive."

—Michael Drayton (1563–1631), English
poet, *The Moon-Calf,* cited in the *Universal
Dictionary of the English Language* (1897)

An old seaman's word used to describe a wind when it draws ahead of the ship, so that she can only just lay her course (i.e., sail the desired heading), with the yards braced up as sharply as possible. Yachtsmen nowadays would call thi "pinching up"; the more common term from the later days of sail would be "sailing close-hauled." From the Old Nors *skamt,* short; when the wind blows progressively from ahead it is said to "shorten."

The word is not related to *scantling,* the dimensions of timber used in ship- and boatbuilding after it has been reduced to the standard size for that type of vessel (Old Northern French *scantillon,* pattern or sample). We now use *scant* in everyday speech to mean barely sufficient, inadequate: "He paid scant regard to the niceties of good manners during his attack on the chairman of the board." Also, a small amount, a stinted supply of. The element of short, confined, restricted is apparent in all these usages.

Scope
To have scope for something

Scope (from the Greek *skopos,* mark, aim) is the length of cable run out when a vessel rides to its anchor. It is the amount (approximately) by which a ship swings about its anchor; its freedom of movement, so to speak. This also exactly describes the figurative use of this phrase; *have scope for something* is to have room to move, to have sufficient opportunity and wherewithal to carry out a particular task.

Scrimshaw

"Some of them have little boxes
of dentistical-looking
implements specially intended
for the skrimshandering
business."

—Herman Melville (1819–1891),
American writer, *Moby Dick* (1851)

Also "scrimshander," "scrimshanker," "scrimshandering," "skrimshander," "skrimshanker." *Scrimshaw,* the more commonly used word, is the carving done by sailors (especially American whalers of the early nineteenth century) on the bones, teeth, and tusks of whales and walruses; shells and ivory were also popular carving media. In essence, it was a hobby to while away the time off watc

carving
on whale tooth

goblet

pastry cutter

clothes peg

To scrimshaw is to make any ingenious and useful article from marine animal parts.

The military uses *scrimshanker* as a term of abuse meaning "shirker," which no doubt is derived from the soldier's perception of what would seem to be a fairly easy existence afloat, if one has the time in which to carve and whittle.

The origin of the word is not certain, but it is likely to be connected with one Admiral Scrimshaw, who was noted for his expertise in this work.

Scrub

From the Dutch *schrubben,* to scratch, to clean with vigour. Originally a nautical word, but taken into everyday speech in the sixteenth century. One interesting usage from eighteenth-century England refers to a reprehensible person, a blackguard, someone to be avoided as a "scrub."

To scrub something

Scrub is seaman's language meaning to cancel, to wipe out; from the days when messages, log readings, etc., were recorded on the slate kept by the officers for this purpose on the quarterdeck of the vessel. The phrase has passed into everyday use; "to scrub something" is to abort it, to erase it and to begin anew.

Scurvy

A disease caused by the lack of vitamin C, brought about by an exclusive diet of salted meat, with no fresh vegetables. The symptoms are spongy flesh, swollen gums, foul breath, and extreme tiredness and debility. Death usually follows if the condition is not treated, but recovery can be remarkably quick if the sufferer is given access to fresh fruit and vegetables.

The disease was prevalent in ships that sailed the long Far Eastern routes, particularly in the sixteenth to eighteenth centuries. Captain Cook in the 1770s was one of the first Royal Navy captains to institute a regimen of antiscorbutic measures, but in fact Dr. James Lind had proved, 20 years earlier, that citrus juices—particularly the juices of lemons, oranges, and, to a lesser extent, limes—were an effective cure for scurvy. Lime juice had, by law, to be carried on all British ships, but it wasn't until the twentieth century that it was discovered that limes had only half the antiscorbutic value of lemons, and that black currants were far superior to both.

It is interesting to note that as long ago as 551, Brendan the Navigator, the Irish monk, is said to have set sail on one of his legendary voyages of discovery with a supply of the roots of blue sea holly, which he believed would safeguard the crew against scurvy.

It was for a long time believed that scurvy was due to the endless use of salt meat aboard ship, but Anson's circumnavigation of 1744 proved this to be a fallacy. When he crossed the Pacific in the *Centurion,* he issued no salt meat at all to the men; instead, the ship's company lived on the livestock that Anson had taken on board before leaving Mexico, and an abundance of fish was caught daily. In addition, the wet season allowed Anson to issue the unusually generous allowance of five pints of quite fresh water daily to every man on board. Nevertheless, during this crossing scurvy claimed the lives of a dozen men each day.

On the *Gloucester,* which accompanied the *Centurion* for most of the crossing, only 77 men and boys were alive when she foundered; the rest of a crew of more than 400 had been

"Whatsoever man … be scurvy or scabbed. . . ."
—Leviticus 21:18–20

four-year circumnavigation, only four men were lost
because of enemy action; virtually all other deaths—
over 1,300 men belonging to Anson's company of six ships—
were due to disease, mainly scurvy. Half the shipwrecks in
history, writes Professor Lloyd (see bibliography), have been
due to crews enfeebled by scurvy.

The word has found its way into our everyday language: we
speak of "a scurvy trick," to mean low, mean, contemptible
behaviour; "a scurvy lad," to mean someone who, in a
jocular sense, is a bit of a villain, one who behaves in a shabby
manner. From the Anglo-Saxon *scurf*, scaly, scabby, but
influenced by the French *scorbut*, scurvy, and perhaps
deriving from the Russian *scrobot*, to scratch.

Scuttle-butt

A shipboard "scuttle" (from the Spanish *escotilla*, a hatchway), as
distinct from the coal scuttle, a word of different origin, is a
hole or formed aperture in the topsides of a vessel. To scuttle
a ship is deliberately to hole it so that it will sink (such as
the scuttling by the Germans of their High Seas Fleet in
Scapa Flow, 1919, to avoid surrender to the British). A "butt"
is a cask.

"We hoysed out our boat, and took up some of them; as also a small hatch, or scuttle rather, belonging to some bark."

—William Dampier (1652–1715), English buccaneer and explorer, *Voyages* (1697)

Sailing ships carried their water in large casks, and a long
voyage demanded that drinking water be sparingly consumed.
The crew obtained their water from a cask provided daily,
but to prevent too much being used, a section of a stave was
sawn out from the cask so that no more than half a butt of
water was available each day. The butt was thus "scuttled."

The term *scuttle-butt* quickly came to mean the shipboard
gossip, news, griping, and so forth that would be passed
around as the watch gathered from time to time at the water
cask. The colloquialism has come to mean gossip
generally.

Seas
The high seas

The open sea, especially that part of the sea beyond a country's declared territorial limit, forming a free highway to the shipping of all nations. The limit used to be defined by the utmost range of a cannon shot, generally accepted as three miles. However, in recent years this limit has been challenged by many countries with a seaboard, with some claiming a territorial limit of up to 200 miles. International maritime conferences have so far failed to settle the issue.

Colloquially, *to be on the high seas* is used as a description of someone who is behaving in a high-handed and cavalier fashion, as if he considered himself beyond the reach of proper authority; like a buccaneer.

Sell
To sell down the river

An expression from the old slaving days; it means to betray, to cheat, to defraud. The chief source of African slaves was for 350 years the West African coast between the River Volta and Mount Cameroon. (Slaves were known to seamen as "blackbirds"; hence the term *blackbirding* to mean slave-trading, especially in Australian Pacific waters in the nineteenth century, ostensibly called "labour recruiting" until it was put down by the Royal Navy in the 1880s.) Slaves were delivered from the hinterland to the coast either by being force-marched through the forest or by being carried downriver on local craft. Slaver ships often went upriver to take on a cargo of slaves.

Another source is the fact that slave owners in the southern states of America frequently got rid of unsatisfactory slaves by selling them to the cotton and sugar plantations of Louisiana that lay farther down the river (i.e., down the Mississippi), where conditions were generally far worse than in the states of the upper Mississippi.

The expression perhaps also owes something to the fact that a short-handed vessel lying in dock would usually secure its complement of crew through the activities of the crimpers. Most of the world's commercial ports of the eighteenth and nineteenth centuries lay on large rivers or estuaries (e.g., London, Shanghai, Rio de Janeiro, and Adelaide). When the shanghaied seaman woke from his alcohol- or drug-induced haze, the ship was usually well on its way down the river to the sea, to begin its voyage. It was by then too late for the seaman to do anything about it; he had been sold down the river.

Served
To be well served

To serve has two nautical meanings: one is to wind spun yarn tightly and closely around a rope that has been wrapped with a canvas sleeve for protection against water rot; the other is to work the ship's guns (the "great guns," as they were called). The gun crew is said to "serve" a gun as they work rapidly through the process of priming, wadding, loading, heaving, pointing, and firing. A gun is well served or not, as the case may be. Colloquially, the phrase means to be treated or dealt with in a proper and satisfying manner, to be given good service.

Shakes
A brace of shakes; in two shakes

When a vessel is steered too close to the wind, its sails shiver or shake; thus, *a brace of shakes* is the seaman's way of saying that something is happening as quickly as it takes for a sail to shiver twice—which is very quickly indeed. The more common expression among landsmen is *two shakes:* "Hang on, I'll be there in two shakes."

No great shakes

"I had my hands full and my head too, just then when he wrote Marino Faliero, so it can be no great shakes."

—George Gordon Byron (1788–1824), English poet, *To Murray*

Shakes are the staves of a cask after it has been taken to pieces. As a seaman's well-being depended upon the integrity of the ship's casks and their contents, a disassembled cask was of little value to him. Hence, attributively, *no great shakes* meant of no use, of little importance.

Shanghai

To abduct a sailor by force, generally with the help of drink or drugs, so as to enlist him aboard a ship other than his own. Particularly common in the nineteenth century on American vessels when crew numbers had to be made up, especially when the fierce reputation of many captains and their bucko mates for ferocity made normal recruitment unlikely. Shanghaied sailors were delivered to the ships by "crimps," who ensnared their otherwise unwilling crew with women, drink, and often drugs, and who were paid by the ship's captain for every man shipped aboard.

The term was widely known in the United States, but its origin is obscure; it may derive from the phrase *to ship him to Shanghai,* i.e., to send him on a long voyage; or it may stem from the Australian word *shanghai,* known by every boy in that country to mean a catapult or "ging," similar in form and use to the much older slingshot. In this sense, unfortunate seamen were "catapulted" off to sea as soon as they were made insensible. However, it is more likely that this Australian slang word for catapult derived from the older nautical usage, as various Australian ports, such as Melbourne, Adelaide, Sydney, and Hobart, were important and well-known shipping centres for merchant sail of many nationalities in the nineteenth century.

To shanghai, in the colloquial sense, means to steal or capture, often by surreptitious means.

Shape
To shape up

The complete colloquialism is "to shape up or ship out." *To shape, in nautical language, is to select a course for the ship to sail; to shape a course* is common parlance among seamen. Figuratively, *to shape up* is to stick to the course, to keep up to expectations. Failure to do so invites the demand to ship out, to quit, to leave the job to someone better qualified. From the Old English *scieppan,* create, shape.

Sheer
To sheer away;
to sheer off

To sheer is to deviate or stray off course in an irregular manner; this might happen because of difficulties with the steering gear, or because of a negligent or inexperienced helmsman. *To sheer off* is a deliberate manoeuvre, in which the vessel is suddenly moved away at an angle to its original course to avoid a collision or some obstacle.

The word is from the German *scheren,* to depart, and is not to be confused with the word as used in "sheer nonsense" or "a sheer slope"; this latter usage is from the Old English *scir,* clear, pure, complete. Metaphorically, the terms *to sheer off* and *to sheer away* mean suddenly to change one's direction of movement, or thrust of argument, because of some perceived obstacle or impediment.

Sheets
Three sheets in the wind

To be very drunk. The sheet is the line (rope or chain) attached to the clew or lower corner of a square sail, or to the aftermost lower corner of a fore-and-aft sail. It controls the extent to which the sail is permitted to capture the wind. If the sheet is let go so that the sail flaps or flags out of control, the sheet is said to be "in the wind," and the vessel will describe a very erratic course.

To have a sheet in the wind is a nautical expression for being a little tipsy; thus the phrase *three sheets in the wind* is to be quite out of control, thoroughly inebriated. (The phrase in America is usually rendered "three sheets *to* the wind.")

Shifty

A shifty person is one who is evasive, unreliable, deceitful, furtive. The phrase is from the name *shifter,* the cook's mate in the old sailing navy. His main job was to shift and wash the salt meat that was stowed in casks in the ship's hold; the meat then had to be steeped in fresh water to remove the salt that it had acquired during its long immersion in brine. No doubt the sailors mistrusted the shifter's devotion to duty, and perhaps they had good reason to, for the residual salt content of their victuals was still at an unhealthily high level. He was, they felt, unreliable; hence "shifty."

Shipshape
All shipshape and Bristol fashion

To have things well organised, in proper order, ready for instant use. The reference is to the methodical way in which a ship and her rigging were equipped, organised, and handled. Such a ship and her crew were said to be "shipshape."

It was necessary for a standardised system of organisation to be adopted, because seamen and officers served in a wide variety of vessels in the course of their careers; in war and in bad weather, the crew had to know instinctively where each item of gear should come to hand.

Bristol fashion refers to the days when Bristol was England's major west coast port, and its shipping had to be maintained in proper good order because the city had no docks and ships were thus left high and dry at low tide. Vessels using the port, therefore, had to be well built and properly maintained to withstand the stresses of taking the ground.

"Keep everything ship-shape, for I must go."
—Alfred, Lord Tennyson (1809–1892), English poet, *Enoch Arden* (1864)

Shore up

From the Dutch *schoar,* a prop, and found in the Anglo-Saxon *scorian,* to project. A shore is a prop or stanchion fixed under a ship's side or bottom, to support her while she is on the stocks or aground. It is also a stout timber used to back up a bulkhead in a ship when excessive pressure is applied to it from the other side, as with a flooded compartment.

Short
To be brought up short

A vessel is "brought up short" when it is caused to stop suddenly by letting go an anchor with too much way or forward motion on the ship. The phrase also describes the result when a ship pitches while at anchor and the cable tautens to such an extent that it holds the bows down at the top of the pitch. In both cases, another common term is *to snub.* The essential element is unexpectedness, curtness.

As a colloquialism, the expression means to stop or deal with someone in an abrupt and summary manner, or to be so dealt with oneself; to be jolted, to be stopped suddenly.

Shot
A long shot

A guess, decision, attempt, or the like, based on long odds and full of risks, unlikely to be right or to succeed but still worth trying. From the firing of a ship's gun at extreme range and hoping to score a hit.

Shove off

From the Anglo-Saxon *scufan,* to shove, and common in other Teutonic languages (e.g., Gothic *afskiuban,* to shove off). Nautically, it means to push clear of, as in a pulling boat or small sailing boat being pushed away by hand (or by boat hook) from a wharf or larger vessel. Colloquially, *to shove off* is to leave, to get going, to start off or away, all usually with a sense of force, immediacy, or urgency.

Sign
To sign on

When a seaman joined a naval ship, he signed his name (or as often made his mark) in the ship's muster book. On this basis he drew his daily provisions during the voyage, and when the ship returned to its home port he was given his pay, for which he signed. When he signed on, the seaman bound himself to the customs and usages of the sea; notably, to the "Thirty-Six Articles of War."

In the merchant service, the seaman signed simply the "Articles," which were the conditions of service he agreed to undertake. They were also signed by the master of the vessel, and they constituted a legal contract binding on both sides.

The "Ship's Articles" specified the rates of pay, scale of provisions, daily hours of work, and—in the days of the Cape Horners—the extremes of latitude beyond which a seaman was not obliged to serve. Discipline on board ship was also set out and governed by the Articles. In a general sense, *to sign on* is to offer oneself for hire, to commit oneself to employment, usually ratified by the signing of a contract between the two parties: "He liked the look of the place and was keen to sign on as the new branch manager."

The "Articles of War," which on a Royal Navy vessel were read out by the captain to the crew at each Sunday service (if the captain chose to "rig church"), laid down both the rules of conduct for seamen and the punishments that could be visited upon them if they transgressed those rules.

The first attempt to codify naval conduct came with the "Black Book of the Admiralty," issued in 1336 and based on the laws of Oleron, which was a system of maritime law enacted by Eleanor of Aquitaine in 1152, and possibly owing something to the earlier Rhodian Law of the Mediterranean. However, many naval captains had already devised their own systems of shipboard punishment; so, to give some uniformity to naval practice, the English government issued the "Articles of War" in 1653, which were then incorporated in the Naval Discipline Act of 1661.

The Articles devoted much effort to spelling out what constituted a crime on any of the English navy vessels and the punishment that could be awarded for each crime. At least one third of these Articles prescribed the death penalty as a proper and lawful punishment.

The comparable regulations in the United States were known as the "Articles for the Government of the Navy." In May 1951, however, Congress introduced the Uniform Code of Military Justice, which now applies to all U.S. armed forces administered by the Department of Defense. By contrast, in Britain, the Army Act of 1955 omitted the "Articles of War," although they are still retained in the Naval Discipline Act of 1956.

Signals
To get one's signals crossed

The first record of a system of communication by flags at sea was in 1753; this method utilised five different flags. By 1857 an International Code of Signals had been introduced, and there was general agreement among the maritime nations to adopt it by the end of the century. Many attempts were made in the intervening years to establish a workable system and to make it acceptable to the warships and merchant ships of the world.

It is easy to understand, therefore, how it would often happen that in the heat of battle, or in an exchange between vessels of different nationalities, mistakes could occur in the fitting of the flags in their correct sequence to the hoist—thus, literally to have one's signals crossed is to have them arranged in the wrong order, with the inevitable confusion or delay in understanding on the part of the receiver. Colloquially, the phrase means to misunderstand someone's intentions, to read the situation wrongly; the emphasis here is on the receiver rather than the sender.

Skids
To be on the skids

The skids, or skid-booms, are the beams that support the deck on which the ship's boats are stowed; frequently a vessel's spare spars were used as support or skids for the boats.

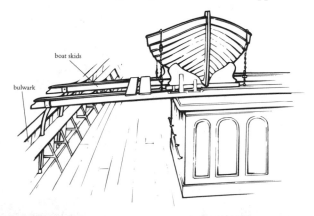

boat skids

bulwark

They were usually kept on the waist deck, with the boats lashed on top of them. Gradually, methods were evolved of lowering the boats (especially as lifeboats) over the ship's side into the sea by sliding them along the skids to the ship's side; these skids are now known as davits.

Colloquially, *to be on the skids* means to be going down in the world, deteriorating rapidly, to be in the process of a downfall; as in "Skid Row." Probably derived from the word *ski* (Old Norse *skith,* snow shoe, also a short length of wood).

Slack-jawed

"Jaw" is the distance between corresponding points on adjacent strands of a rope. A hard-laid rope will show a shorter jaw than a softer-laid rope. When a rope has been much used and the lay or strands have become slack, the distance between corresponding points will have increased, and the rope is then said to be "slack-jawed" or "long-jawed." It is tempting to conjecture that the metaphor—to be slack-jawed with surprise, to be taken aback, gaping in bewilderment—owes something to the nautical term.

Slate
A clean slate

A slate was kept on deck, on which were recorded the courses and distances run during the period of a watch. At the end of the watch, this information was recorded in the deck-log and the slate was then wiped clean so that it was ready for use by the officer keeping the next watch. The phrase has come to mean that past actions and occurrences are to be forgotten and that a new start can be made, i.e., the slate has been wiped clean.

Slew

A nautical word meaning to turn something on its own axis; to cause to swing round or to swerve awkwardly. Also *slewed,* seaman's slang for drunk. The origin of the word is unknown. It is in wide usage in everyday speech: "When

the car hit the oily patch, it slewed across to the other side
and slammed into the side of the shop."

Slip   From the Anglo-Saxon *slipor,* slippery.

To give one the slip   *To slip* is to release the inboard end of mooring lines
securing a ship to the bollards or mooring cleats on shore. It
was sometimes necessary for a vessel to be able to clear its
berth immediately if it were exposed to untoward weather;
to do so, the lines were slipped from the bitts inboard. If at
anchor and slipping was necessary, the anchor cable was
buoyed before letting it slip through the hawse-pipe, so that
anchor and cable could be recovered at a later date when
conditions were more favourable.

In the metaphorical sense, "to give one the slip" is to steal
away unobserved, undetected, so as to elude pursuit.

To let slip   *To slip,* or *to let slip,* is to release the inboard ends of the
mooring lines that secure a ship to the bollards or mooring
cleats on shore, or to the mooring buoy. This is often done
by using a slip rope, the end of which is passed through the
ring of the mooring buoy and brought back on board. The
ship is then easily freed from her mooring when the rope is
let go from inboard and hauled back through the mooring
ring.

As an expression, *to let slip* is to say or reveal something
quickly but unintentionally: "He let slip that his wife had
been criticising me for my talkativeness"; also to release
something quickly and efficiently (as in Shakespeare's
". . . let slip the dogs of war"—*Julius Caesar* III.i). The
element common to all these expressions ("to give the slip,"
"to slip away," etc.) is that of swiftness, speed without fuss.

To slip off/away   *To slip off* is to move away quietly, without fuss and bother,
so as to give little if any notice of one's departure. From the

fact that a vessel could effect a sudden and efficient departure by slipping her cable after having buoyed the anchor, and running to open sea, as in a bad storm while anchored near the shore.

Slush fund   Also "slush money"; a fund of money for use in political campaigning, as for the production of propaganda, posters, news releases, and the like. The term has gained some notoriety because a slush fund is usually kept secret, out of the public gaze; in twentieth-century politics, the amounts can be very large, leaving many people to wonder about the origin of these monies, and whether they are used for the purposes of bribery, corruption, or other unsavoury ends.

The origin of the term itself, and its meaning, is perfectly innocuous. "Slush" was the fat collected from meat after it had been boiled in the coppers of naval ships. This slush was one of the perquisites of the ship's cook; he usually sold it to the purser, who made it into candles (the "pusser's dip," a long-lasting candle made by repeatedly dipping the central core or wick into the fat and allowing it to congeal).

Slush was also the name given to the grease (usually mixed with linseed oil, tallow soap, and any remaining fat) used for rubbing down masts, spars, and rigging to help preserve them against water-rot. Hence the name for partly melted snow, and for fat, grease, and slops in general that are discarded from the kitchen.

The transition in meaning from an accepted practice in the sailing navy to what has become a questionable practice in present-day politics is a curious one, and bears witness to the pervasive nature of nautical language and customs. The connection is the fact that the refuse—the slush—collected by the "slushy" (the ship's cook) was distasteful, repulsive, to be kept apart, away, hidden (in the sense of securely stowed); hence the secret and somewhat abhorrent nature of political

or commercial slush funds, the operators of which do not **155**
generally want its existence to be made known or seen.
Probably from the Norwegian *sluss,* mud, mire.

Smart money   The term used in the old days (seventeenth century) of
the sailing navy to describe a pension awarded for wounds
acquired on active service. It was issued on a sliding scale
according to rank and the extent of the wound. The term
refers to the fact that compensation is based on the severity
of the wound and the degree of pain (the "smarting") it
caused.

Nowadays the expression is a colloquialism that alludes to
the knowing way in which informed persons make a
prediction or lay a bet, often in opposition to others who
are influenced by general opinion.

Snob   Originally a shoemaker or shoe repairer on board ship, in
the eighteenth century. The transition of meaning between
that of cobbler and that of someone who affects airs of
social importance and exclusiveness is quite obscure. This
latter sense—that of a social upstart—is a mid-nineteenth-
century development.

"That which we call a snob, by
any other name would still be
snobbish."

—William Makepeace Thackeray
(1811–1863), English novelist, The Book
of Snobs (1847)

Snottie   *Snottie* is naval slang for a midshipman, an apprentice officer.
In the early days of fighting sail, midshipmen went to sea at
a very early age, often as youngsters barely newly breeched,
and their nickname is said to come from their habit of
wiping their noses on their sleeves. Tradition has it that
Nelson ordered three buttons to be sewn on the sleeves of
midshipmen to prevent this unseemly practice.

To be snotty is to be angry, querulous, easily irritated; from
the fact that the extreme youth of the nautical snottie made
him susceptible to temper and tears—until the unerring
hand of naval discipline showed him the value of accepting
all things to do with nautical life.

Snub　From the Old Norse *snubba,* to check or rebuke; essentially to shorten, as in the nautical usage to suddenly stop a rope or cable from running out any further by taking extra turns around a bollard, etc., or by applying a cable stopper or some other means of braking its movement. A vessel snubs when she is brought up short by her anchor while pitching in a seaway.

Metaphotically, when we snub someone we give a sudden check or restraint to an assumed acquaintanceship or friendship; the disdain and contempt expressed in the snub puts a sudden end to further social intercourse.

So long　The sailor's farewell: "goodbye till we meet again." The expression was an integral part of the sailor's vocabulary; Captain Frank Bullen ends his *The Cruise of the Cachalot* (1910) with it. Now a common part of the landlubber's language.

SOS　The internationally agreed distress call made by a ship requiring assistance; it was adopted in 1908. These three letters were chosen because in Morse Code they were easy to read and transmit: three dots, three dashes, three dots. These letters, contrary to popular belief, do not stand for "save our souls" or "save our ship." The expression now means any call for help.

Sound
To sound somebody out

"His Holiness, however, on being sounded on the subject by the Spanish Ambassador in Rome, declined."

—*The Evening Standard* (English newspaper), October 3, 1885

To sound, from the ancient Sanskrit *sond,* messenger, is to determine the depth of water beneath the vessel's keel, using either the hand lead line or, in more recent times, electronic devices, such as sonar. *To sound somebody out* implies that one is going to plumb his or her depths, as it were, to determine what he or she thinks of a certain matter; to obtain an opinion, often so as to solicit approval or cooperation.

Span
Spick and span

Of nautical origin, meaning quite new, entirely new, of recent manufacture. In the days of wooden sailing ships, a "spic" was a nail or spike, and a "span" was a chip of wood just struck from a length of timber. A "spick and span" new ship was therefore one in which every nail and chip was new, as from being freshly built. Colloquially, to be all neat, clean, bright, and tidy, exactly as in brand new.

From Old Norse *span,* chip, and Swedish *spik,* nail, spike. Other versions are "span-new," "bran-span-new," and "bran-spanking-new," which were once very common expressions in Australia and England.

Spanking
To be spanking along

Spanking means brisk, lively. The "spanker" is the fore-and-aft sail set on a gaff on the mizzenmast of a three-masted vessel, or on the aftermost mast of a vessel with four or more masts, such as a four-masted barque (or

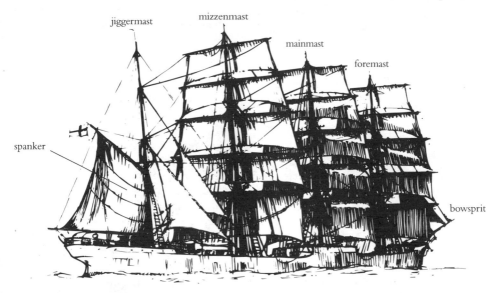

"bark") or the five-masted full-rigged ship, the remarkable *Preussen*. Vessels with one or two masts do not carry a spanker as such.

This sail was set principally to take advantage of a following wind; it proved to be so useful in this regard, and also as an aid to steering, that it replaced entirely the mizzen course (the lowest square sail once set on the mizzenmast, corresponding to the mainsail on the mainmast).

Hence, the phrase *to be spanking along* is, both nautically and colloquially, to be moving at a brisk and lively pace, with all stops out. A wind producing this turn of events is known as a "spanking breeze" or a "spanker." From its imitative relationship with a resonant slap; but also cognate with the Scottish *spang,* to move rapidly, and also possibly the Portuguese *espancar,* to strike.

Spirit
To spirit away

Originally a phrase in nautical usage, to mean the abduction of young boys in England for transportation to the West Indies plantations, where they were put to work as slaves. The reference was to the fact that they were taken in secret, as though they had been supernaturally removed. The expression is used as a metaphor carrying much the same ground-sense: to carry away or remove something or someone secretly and suddenly, as if by magic.

Squeegee

The familiar rubber-edged "broom" used for sweeping water from windows, vehicle windscreens, and the like, after they have been washed. Originally a nautical word, with the variation "squilgee"; it referred to the swab used for washing and cleaning the decks, and is a corruption of "squeege," which itself is a colloquialism for "squeeze."

Stand

From the Anglo-Saxon *standan,* and common to the Teutonic languages; derived from the Latin *stare,* to stay, to be at, and the Sanskrit *stha,* to be at. Found in a number of originally

To stand by

A common expression, as in "Stand by for further instructions," "Stand by for the weather report"; to wait in a state of readiness, be ready to give assistance, if needed. From the Anglo-Saxon *stanan,* with similar cognates found in other Teutonic tongues.

A very common word in nautical language; found also in nautical expressions such as "to stand in," "standing block," "to stand off and on," "to stand on," "to stand up," and others. It is interesting that a "standby"—which is now a supporter, an adherent, something kept in readiness, a fall-back—was originally an attendant ship, a smaller vessel that stood by and kept in company with a larger vessel, to act as messenger, escort, signal repeater, and the like.

Stand–offish

From the nautical term *to stand off* (to keep away from the shore or from another vessel). When a ship nears the land but wishes to wait for clearer conditions, or for a pilot, she will sail alternately toward and away from her destination until she is able to proceed safely; that is, she will stand "off and on." The expression is applied colloquially to people: *to be stand-offish* is to be unfriendly, unsociable, snobbish, in the sense of deliberately keeping away from one's fellows.

Stave
To stave in

"The feared disorders that might ensue thereof have been an occasion that divers times all the wine in the city hath been staved."

—George Sandys (1578–1644), English poet and traveler, *Travels* (1615)

To stave in something is to break it up. Specifically, it means to break in the planking of a vessel to sink her, or to drive in the head of a cask, especially if it contains spirits, to prevent the crew getting at it in the case of shipwreck (otherwise the men would become unmanageable). A boat is stove in, a cask is staved in. Staves are the component "planks" of a cask after it has been dismantled or knocked down.

To stave off

To stave off is to keep the boat's side away from a jetty or some floating object by thrusting with a pole, boathook, or some similar implement. The intention is to prevent collision. As a metaphor, the expression carries the same meaning: to keep off or ward off, by force or evasion or some other means, some undesired event. *Stave* here is related to *staff*, from the Old English *staef*, stick or pole.

Stern
A stern aspect

Related to *steer*, from the Old Norse *stjorn*, steering. The stern of a vessel is its hind- or aftermost part, the external rear section of a ship's hull. It is usually a quite bluff conclusion to a vessel's lines, and this abruptness of appearance is reflected in the phrase *a stern aspect*, meaning an angry or at least unfriendly and forbidding face or appearance.

Stopper
To put a stopper on things

A stopper is a short length of rope or chain, firmly secured at one end, used as a temporary measure to take the strain off a cable that is under tension; as in "anchor-stopper," "deck-stopper," "sheet-stopper." Colloquially, a stopper is anything that puts a stop to something, for example, a sudden rainstorm spoiling a barbecue party.

Stow it

"On Wednesday we had finished the stowage of the hold."

—Captain James Cook (1728–1779), English navigator and explorer, *Third Voyage* (1784)

Sailors' slang for shut up, stop it. From the maritime usage, to arrange goods compactly in a ship's hold or between decks; more generally, to put away, stop, as in "stow the hammocks," or "stow that talk." From the Dutch *stouwen*, to pack or press in.

Straggler

The old-time description of a deserting seaman, one who has had "R" for "Run" put alongside his name on his ship's muster-roll. Civilians-at-large were paid a reward, plus conduct money, for reporting him to the authorities, and the seaman himself was charged with "straggling," the equivalent of desertion. Nowadays the word means simply one who falls behind, who fails to keep up with others; also to wander about, ramble.

Stretcher

Originally a piece of wood fixed sideways across the bottom of a pulling boat against which the rowers could brace their feet; also a short length of wood used for spreading apart the corners of each end of a hammock when it was being used. The modern sense of the word—a light folding bed, such as a camp stretcher or first-aid stretcher—derives from the nautical ground-sense of hauling taut, or of drawing out or extending oneself, as in rowing.

Stuff

A word that has enjoyed a remarkably wide sense-development. Originally it meant "tow" (pronounced "toe"), the fibre of flax, hemp, or jute, prepared for spinning. This sense is still preserved in the nautical term *small stuff,* meaning any yarn, cord, or line less than one inch in circumference; and in *stuff,* meaning a composition of materials used to smear or pay the sides and bottom on a ship as a protection against worm. The mixture usually included turpentine, varnish, tar, oils, and various other ingredients. The stuffing-box of a propeller shaft (or piston rod on a steam engine) is an adjustable gland containing (originally) teased-out oakum which, when compressed by the gland nut, provided a reasonably watertight or steamtight fit or joint.

The word now refers simply to the material of which anything is made. In the leather and fabric industries, *stuff* has a particular meaning, but in everyday usage the meaning varies widely, often being determined only by context. From the Old French *estoffer,* to provide, and ultimately from the Latin *stuppa,* tow.

Sweep
To make a clean sweep

When a man-o'-war went into action, the crew cleared the decks of unwanted gear, including the movable bulkheads (walls) that formed the divisions between various cabins and spaces on the gun decks. To do so was *to make a clean sweep*. Also, if a broadside of shot wreaked enough havoc on the enemy's decks, so as to kill or injure a large number of the crew working there, the guns were said to have made *a clean sweep*.

The expression has found its way into a number of usages, some associated with gaming (gambling at the table), horseracing, and so on. Colloquially, *to make a clean sweep* is to dispose completely of anything; to get rid of materials, methods, or staff that are regarded as obsolete or redundant; to get rid of entirely: "By the end of the week, the new manager had made a clean sweep of all the lazy and inefficient people in his department."

There is a story, probably apocryphal, that the Dutch admiral Marten Tromp hoisted a broom to his masthead after a victory over the British in the English Channel in 1652; if true, his meaning is obvious. From the Middle English *swepe,* to sweep.

T

Tailor made Cigarettes made in a factory. This was the sailor's derisory description of the tinned tobacco that was introduced to replace the leaf tobacco that each seaman had learned to roll and cure aboard ship. Because smoking was restricted to certain times and places, most seamen preferred to chew their tobacco; consequently, they made their individual issues up into a *perique* (usually corrupted to "prick"), a one-pound pack of rolled, bound, and cured tobacco leaf. (*Perique* was the French name for a rich-flavoured tobacco grown in Louisiana.) The expression *tailor made* was once in wide circulation, particularly following both world wars, but the generally improved standard of living since the war years has made the commercially produced cigarette so common and readily available that the "roll-your-own" type is more the exception than the rule.

Tampon Nowadays a plug or dressing of cotton or similar material used to plug or staunch the flow of blood from a wound; also a sanitary device for absorbing the menstrual flow. Of nautical origin, unlikely though it might seem; from the French *tompion, tampion,* a wooden plug or stopper placed in the muzzle of a cannon, when not in use, to keep out seawater. The English word *tap,* as in "bath-tap," is also cognate with this French word.

Tarred
Tarred and feathered

"Tarred and feathered and
carried on a cart
By the women of
Marblehead. . . ."
—J. G. Whittier (1807–1892), American
poet, *Skipper Ireson's Ride* (1857)

A punishment that involves being stripped to the skin, painted with tar, and then rolled in feathers. It is first recorded as being applied as a punishment at sea in the *Laws of Richard Coeur de Lion, Third Crusade* (1189): "A robber convicted of theft shall be shorn like a hired fighter, and boiling tar shall be poured over his head, and feathers from a pillow shall be shaken out over his head." This form of retribution against wrongdoers is still practised in some primitive communities today (one wonders how the victim survives the burns to his body). Once known as "painting the lion," an old nautical term of much the same meaning. The practice was not unknown in America, as noted by Francis Gros in *A Classical Dictionary of the Vulgar Tongue* (1785).

Tell
To tell off

To tell off is to detail each man in a watch to some particular duty or position in the ship. The essential sense is to enumerate, to mention one thing after another, to separate each individual person from the whole or group and to assign to each one a particular task. When the watch was mustered, or at some other convenient time in the ship's routine, each man would be "told off" by the officer of the watch, usually one of the ship's mates. Colloquially, *to tell off* is to scold, to rebuke severely, to itemise one after another the victim's flaws and faults; hence, *to be told off.*

Telltale

Originally, the compass (sometimes called the "overhead compass" or "hanging compass") hanging face downward from the beams in the captain's cabin, so as to show him the direction of the ship's head (its compass course) without the need to go on deck. Nowadays the word *telltale* on board ship is used generally to indicate any mechanical contrivance that repeats or reproduces useful information. It is also the word for the lengths of ribbon, wool, etc., attached to the shrouds of a sailboat to indicate

airflow. Colloquially, a "telltale" is something that reveals or
discloses, or betrays what is not intended to be known, as in
"a telltale blush."

Tidy   *To be in tide* is to be in season, to be timely, as in eventide
and springtide. To do things at their proper time or season is
to ensure that they are done in an orderly manner, in the
same way that the tides ebb and flow in a regular rhythm;
hence, by association, the word *tidy* came to mean
methodical, neatly done, well arranged. The connection with
ocean tides is obvious; *tidy* is an adverbial formation from
tide.

Time
To serve one's time

"He is a good time-server that
improves the present for God's
glory and his own salvation."

—Thomas Fuller (1608–1661), English
preacher, *The Holy State and the Profane
State* (1642)

From the early days when young men joined the British
navy with a view to becoming naval officers. Their rank was
next below that of sublieutenant, but originally they were
petty officers under the immediate command of the bosun
(boatswain). Many of these young men went to
sea as a captain's servant, and after three years' service
they were rated as midshipmen. Following another
three years' sea-time service, they were eligible to sit for
their lieutenant's examination; hence the origin of the
expression *to serve one's time:* to put in the period of duty
and service that qualified one for the next promotional
examination.

Colloquially, to put in the necessary time in a place or
position, as in an apprenticeship or probationary period. A
"time-server" is one who puts in this necessary time for the
sake of salary, retirement benefits, or such; one who waits for
this to happen.

Perhaps one of the best-known examples of time-serving
was the sixteenth-century Vicar of Bray, who managed to
retain his position in his Berkshire parish despite the
religious upheavals that marked the reigns of Henry VIII,
Edward VI, Mary, and Elizabeth I, all of which occurred

during the vicar's lifetime. This gentleman is commemorated in the song named after him.

Toe the line

To submit to discipline or regulations, to come into line with the rest. From the fact that when the captain of a naval ship had his crew mustered for inspection (called "beating to divisions"), the ship's company lined the quarterdeck, the gangways, and the forecastle, with each group of men lined up along the deck, where their officers made them stand upright, keep in order, and "toe the line" (stand in a straight line along the appointed seams in the deck). Beating to divisions was an important ceremony, charged with tradition and discipline; toeing the line was an important element of that discipline. The expression is widely used in everyday speech and conveys the same sort of meaning: to conform, to behave according to the rules.

Top
To blow one's top

To become very angry, to lose one's temper. There are at least two suggestions as to the origin of this term. One is that it is from the early days of oil-wells in the United States, when gas and oil were struck during the drilling process and the (frequently) unexpected eruption caused the derrick or drill-rig to blow or collapse. The other refers to the blowing-out of a topsail, and its subsequent loss, during a storm.

This second suggested origin is the one to be preferred, simply because of the enormously widespread nature of nautical metaphor and the equally sparse availability of the oil-well metaphor. Furthermore, the possessive pronoun "his" refers more obviously to the ship's captain than it does to any particular person logically connected with a drilling rig (note the curious nautical distinction between "she" the ship and "he" the captain or master, or "old man": *she* was invoked when a ship's performance was referred to; *he* was used when the seaman spoke of ship management).

Top drawer Anything that is "top drawer" is of the best quality, the finest available. The origin of this expression dates from the practice of carrying the ship's papers always and only in the topmost drawer of the desk in the captain's study or the vessel's chart room. Thus, if it were ever necessary to abandon ship, the captain or one of his officers would instantly and automatically know where to retrieve these important documents, because of their being kept only in that one place.

Tornado An English corruption of the Spanish *tronada,* from the Latin, *tonare,* to thunder, and the Sanskrit *tan,* to resound. One of the elements of the Spanish word is *tornar,* to turn, which is descriptive of the violent, thunderous whirlwind that occurs over land and sea in moderately low latitudes. Its winds are capable of wreaking great havoc. The word came into English through the days of privateering and piracy by the Spanish in the Caribbean.

Touch
Touch and go To *touch and go* is to run a vessel aground but to refloat her almost immediately; it is to graze the bottom very slightly, in such a way as not to cause any serious damage or even check the vessel's progress through the water. An originally nautical term, which now means metaphorically a narrow escape, something that was precarious and risky; also something that almost didn't quite come off, as a celebration party or the like.

Trice
To do something in a trice

"In a trice the turnpike men Their gates wide open threw."
—William Cowper (1731–1800), English poet, *John Gilpin* (1782)

"To trice up" is the operation of hauling and lashing to make something more secure, as, for example, in lashing a seaman to the gratings in preparation for a flogging. *Trice* means to tie up, to make fast smartly and without waste of time, in a seamanlike manner. Hence, *to do something in a trice* is to do it in an instant, as a knowledgeable and experienced seaman would. From the verb *trice,* related to the Dutch *trijsen,* to hoist. The old verb *trice* meant at one pull, at one haul; to pluck or snatch; hence the modern usage implying immediacy.

Trick
To do a trick

"...And all I ask is a merry yarn
from a laughing fellow rover,
And quiet sleep and a sweet dream
when the long trick's over."

—John Masefield (1878–1967),
English poet laureate, "Sea Fever," from
Salt-Water Ballads (1902)

A "trick" was the spell of duty done by the helmsman at the wheel or tiller. A "regular trick" varied in time between half an hour and one hour, depending on the size of the crew and the prevailing weather conditions. The ability to steer was a prime requisite for a seaman (an able-bodied seaman was one who could "hand, reef, and steer"), and a skillful trick at the wheel was something to be admired.

Colloquially, one who pulls off a delicate task with skill and perhaps daring is said to have done, or to have pulled, a "neat trick."

True blue

A well-known expression in the English-speaking world; as a colloquialism, it is a testament to someone's faithfulness, unswerving loyalty, and honesty.

The term came to be applied to the seamen of the Royal Navy, who felt (rightly enough) that their willingness to endure the natural hazards of the sea and the rigours and dangers of battle, all of which were a part of the seaman's daily life afloat, was a sufficient measure of their unwavering loyalty to crown and country. In this they were, of course, absolutely right. Basil Lubbock, in his book *The Blackwall Frigates* (1924), tells an interesting anecdote concerning an encounter between the monarch and one of his sailors:

> On one occasion King George was inspecting the embarkation of some cavalry before a large number of spectators, when a jolly tar, who was described as "three sheets in the wind and a-brimful of loyalty," forced his way to the side of the king and held out a quart mug full of porter. Then after "tongueing his quid, unshipping his skyscraper and hitching up his canvas" [i.e., spitting out his chew of tobacco,

removing his hat, and hitching up his trousers] he expressed the hope that His Majesty would not refuse a drink with a "true blue"... whereby they toasted the army and the navy.

The origin of the term stems from the reputation that the city of Coventry had long enjoyed for the quality and fastness of its dyeing. For hundreds of years, the people of this city had been at the forefront of the wool trade and in particular were renowned for their skill in producing dyes that were both fast and consistent in colour. "Coventry Blue" was one of the best-known of these dyes.

Hence, any individual who exhibited these same qualities—of steadfastness and trueness—could be called a "true blue." To many people, the seamen of the king's navy were a prime example of true-blue qualities.

Try
To try; to try out

"The wylde corne, beinge in shape and greatnesse lyke to the good, if they be mengled [mingled] with great difficultie wyll be tryed out."

—Sir Thomas Elyot (?1499–1546), English scholar, *Boke Named the Governour* (1531)

"The fire seven times tried this: Seven times tried that judgment is."

—William Shakespeare (1564–1616), *The Merchant of Venice,* act 2, scene 9

To try was the old seafaring term that described the attempt by a sailing vessel, during a severe storm, to remain in the trough of the waves by reducing sail; sometimes done under bare poles; to ride or lie a-try; hence the origin of the trysail, a sail of much reduced size used by sailing vessels (especially small craft) in place of the mainsail during a storm. *To try back* means to veer or change direction slightly.

The expression *to try out* is from the days of whaling (which itself goes back into antiquity). Whale oil was obtained from the blubber by boiling it in the "try-works," a very large iron pot set in brickwork on board the vessel; this process was known as "trying out the oil." The try-pot was set going by a wood fire, and then maintained with pieces of blubber from which the oil had already been extracted. The resulting overall stench on such a whaling ship was peculiar to the industry and quite permanent. The metaphor *to try out* derives from the whaling usage; it means to test, to experiment, to compete, as for a position; to make an attempt or endeavour. From the French *trier,* to sift or sort, to separate the good from the bad; to test, to prove.

Trying
A trying time

A colloquialism meaning a testing time, when one may be annoyed, irritated, distressed; where one's patience is put to the test or one's mettle is proved. From the nautical manoeuvre "to lie a-try," which meant to lie-to in heavy weather, usually under reduced sail and sometimes under bare poles; also known as "trying." Sails specifically developed for lying-to under these conditions were called "trysails" (pronounced "tri-s'ls").

Turn
Turn and turn about

The same as "hot bunking": the use of the same bunk for sleeping by seamen in opposite watches; practised only in vessels that offered restricted accommodations, such as submarines. The shoregoing version of hot bunking is known as "Box and Cox," from the nineteenth-century farce *Box and Cox* by J. M. Morton (1811–1891), in which the deceitful lodging-house landlady Mrs. Bouncer lets the same room to two men, Box and Cox, who unknown to each other occupy it alternately. One of the two is out at work all day, the other all night; each man pays full rates for the room. The play was very successfully produced in 1847. Hence the colloquial usage meaning one after the other, each taking his turn.

Sailing ships of the nineteenth century provided sufficient space in the fo'c'sle for the men's bunks, although it was always cramped, dirty, and usually damp. Of course, in the Royal Navy of an earlier period, each man had his regulation 14 inches of space in which to sling his hammock from the beams of the lower deck.

Turnout
A good turnout

"... there was a good turn-out of members."

—*Field Magazine,* October 8, 1885

"The morning commences with the watch on deck 'turning to' at daybreak and washing down, scrubbing, and swabbing the decks."

—Richard Henry Dana (1815–1882), American writer and jurist, *Two Years Before the Mast* (1840)

A "turnout" is a showing, a gathering, the result of some organising of events, such as a party or a celebration of some kind. The colloquialism stems from the order to sailors to "turn-in" to their bunks at the end of their watch, then to "turn-out" at the beginning of their work period, and to "turn-to" at their appointed tasks.

The turnout was the total complement of men available and fit enough for watch-duty. Hence the modern-day meaning of a "good turnout," which refers to a gathering somewhat larger, more pleasing, or more impressive than had been expected.

V

Veer
To veer away; to veer off

To veer, in the sense of turning or shifting to another direction, as does the wind. From the Latin *vertere,* to turn; but the nautical usage, to slacken or let out (as in "veer the anchor chain") is from the early Dutch *vieren,* to let out. Colloquially, when one veers away from something, one is shifting direction, as is a ship when it veers in its course.

Victuals

The old name for food, provisions; from the Latin *victualia,* provisions. The term has long been linked with maritime history, since the days of exploratory voyages beyond sight of land, when the provisioning and storing of food on board ship became a matter of considerable importance. Victualling ships were always required to supply a fleet when it was likely to be at sea for a lengthy period.

> "There remained in company only our own squadron and our two victuallers."
>
> —Admiral George Anson (1697–1762), English naval commander and explorer, *A Voyage Round the World* (1748),

The Victualling Board of the Royal Navy, in its various forms over a long period of time, was responsible for the purchase, preservation, and distribution to ships of food, slops, and other provisioning requirements. The official on board ship whose task was to issue rations to the seamen was known as the purser (ultimately from the Greek *byrsa,* hide or leather, a bag or container, hence a purse).

> "To see that the crew properly victual themselves."
>
> —*Field Magazine,* December 24, 1887

Vogue

To be in vogue; to be the vogue

"The vogue of the hansom in Paris was transient."

—*The Daily Telegraph* (English newspaper), March 15, 1886

From the French *voguer,* to be carried forward on the water by oar or by sail, or to move with the tide or the current. When something is "in vogue," or "is the vogue" (usually fashion, or some expression in speech), it is copied by those who wish to be thought up-to-date. The phrase is no longer in vogue with seamen today.

Waft

"But soft, who wafts us yonder?"
—William Shakespeare (1564–1616), *The Comedy of Errors*, act 2, scene 2

A now obsolete nautical term, meaning to convey merchant shipping, to provide protection to such a convoy. Merchant ships in time of war were *wafted* from place to place by *wafters,* what today we would call escort vessels. The word was widely used in this sense in early nautical literature, but now it means to bear or carry through the air or over the water, as in "The sound of singing was wafted on the gentle breeze"; to bear or carry lightly, as in "He wafted her away from the noisy throng." From the Dutch *wahten,* to watch, guard; found in the Middle English *waughter,* armed escort vessel.

Wash-out

Colloquially, a fiasco, a failure, a nonstarter; also to cancel, to disregard; from the times when naval signal messages were taken down on a slate, which was wiped or washed clean when the message had been dealt with. The metaphor is in wide use in everyday language.

Weather
To be under the weather

To feel unwell, out of sorts, either as a result of illness or, less often, untoward weather. Literally, it means to be in the path of bad weather, made worse perhaps by the possibility of having a lee shore. It is also a colloquialism for being inebriated.

The phrase has an obvious connection with *mal-de-mer;* sailors are traditionally lightly contemptuous of landsmen who succumb to seasickness, which is the visible symptom of being under the influence of the weather (although it is worth noting that Lord Nelson himself freely admitted to being seasick for a day or two whenever he went to sea).

Whacked

Originally, "whack" was the serving-out of the cooked food in each mess in the days of sail in the British navy. Nowadays a quite well-known colloquialism in British and Australian usage, to mean exhausted or defeated: "I am quite whacked from all that work on the squash court." Derived from the fact that one's whack was the exact amount, the limit, beyond which there was no more (in this sense, the squash player has used up all her energy—there is nothing left). American usage is similar, with the added meaning of crazy, often seen in the form "whacky," "wacky," or "wacko."

Whip
To whip something up

"The whip passes rapidly toward the wreck, and arriving there the sailors make fast the tail-block in accordance with the directions on the tally-board, and show a signal to the shore."

—*Scribner's Magazine,* January 1880

A whip is a small tackle (block and pulley arrangement) used for light tasks; usually comprising a single rope rove through a single block, and used for hoisting, pulling, and the like. Combinations can be made so as to exert more power, as in a double whip, whip-upon-whip, and such. *To whip up* was literally the act of hoisting quickly and without delay; hence the colloquial usage meaning to create or organise quickly and efficiently.

Yarn
To spin a yarn

"[He] who has yarned aforetime 'On the Fo'k'sle Head' and 'Round the Galley Fire.'"
—*The Daily Telegraph* (English newspaper), December 29, 1885

To tell a story. From the sailor's habit of telling stories and reminiscing to pass the time while engaged in deckwork such as teasing pieces of old rope into short lengths of oakum, or working up rope-yarn into more serviceable small stuff. Spun yarn had a variety of uses on board a wind-driven vessel, such as stropping sails to enable them to be hoisted while still bundled (furled), or for a variety of kinds of seizing, serving, and the like. The metaphor is from the idea of stretching, teasing out, putting to good use, and so on.

Youngster

Originally a nautical usage, to refer to the midshipmen (the "young gentlemen") who messed in the after cockpit on the orlop deck, a nonfighting deck immediately above the hold, and consequently one that was dingy, damp, and very small, beset by foul odours from the bilge, rotting rope, spilled gin and beer, and the lingering odours of fried food. The other occupants of this mess were the master's mates, the surgeon's mates, and the captain's clerk, most of whom were known as "oldsters."

Professor Lloyd (see bibliography) points out that the *Sea Grammar* (1627) of Captain John Smith (the same John Smith who founded the colony of Virginia) defines the sailor as "the older man who hoists the sails and the younker is the younger man called foremast man to take in top sails etc." Captain Smyth, in his *Sailor's Word Book* of some two centuries later, gives both terms, *youngster* and *younker,* and defines them as referring to "a volunteer of the first-class, and a general epithet for a stripling in the service." An English formation influenced by the Dutch *yonker* and *yong heer,* young sir.

Bibliography

The following is a selected list of books that deal with topics covered by this volume. A list of dictionaries consulted for etymologies and historical citations (where appropriate) appears at the end of the bibliography.

Selected Sources

Admiralty Manual of Seamanship. Volumes 1–3. London, 1972.

Chapman, Charles F. *Piloting, Seamanship and Small Boat Handling*. 53d ed. New York: Motor Boating and Sailing, 1967.

Clarkson, Henry. *The Yachtsman's A–Z*. Newton Abbot, England: David & Charles, 1979.

Dana, Richard Henry. *Two Years Before the Mast*. Reprint ed. London: Heron Books, 1968.

Falconer, William. *An Universal Dictionary of the Marine*. Reprint ed. Newton Abbot, England: David & Charles, 1970.

Gaby, Captain James. *Mate in Sail*. Artarmon, New South Wales: Antipodean, 1974.

Garrett, Richard. *The British Sailor*. London: Wayland, 1974.

Greenhill, Basil. *The Merchant Schooners*. Revised ed. New York: A. M. Kelley, 1968.

Hakluyt, Richard. *Voyages and Documents*. Janet Hampden, ed. London: Oxford University Press, 1958.

Hampshire, A. Cecil. *Just an Old Navy Custom*. London: William Kimber, 1979.

Harland, John. *Seamanship in the Age of Sail: An Account of the Sailing Man-of-War, 1600–1860*. London: Conway Maritime Press, 1984.

Kemp, Peter. *The British Sailor: A Social History of the Lower Deck*. London: Dent, 1970.

Kemp, Peter, ed. *The Oxford Companion to Ships and the Sea*. London: Oxford University Press, 1976.

Landstrom, Bjorn. *The Ship: A Survey of the History of the Ship from the Primitive Raft to the Nuclear-Powered Submarine*. Michael Phillips, transl. London: Allen & Unwin, 1961.

Lewis, Michael. *A Social History of the Navy, 1793–1815*. London: Allen & Unwin, 1960.

Lind, Lew. *Sea Jargon*. Sydney, Australia, 1982.

Lloyd, Christopher. *The British Seaman 1200–1860: A Social Survey*. London: Collins, 1968.

The Lore of Ships. New York: Crescent, 1975.

Marryat, Frederick. *Mr. Midshipman Easy*. Reprint ed. London: J. M. Dent, 1959.

Masefield, John. *Sea Life in Nelson's Time*. Reprint ed. London: Conway Maritime Press, 1971.

Morton, Henry. *The Wind Commands: Sailors and Sailing Ships in the Pacific*. Reprint ed. University of Queensland Press, 1980.

O'Brian, Patrick. The "Jack Aubrey" novels:
Master and Commander (1970); *Post Captain* (1972); *HMS Surprise* (1973); *The Mauritius Command* (1977); *Desolation Island* (1978); *The Fortunes of War* (1979); *The Surgeon's Mate* (1980); *The Ionian Mission* (1981); *Treason's Harbour* (1983); *The Far Side of the World* (1984); *The Reverse of the Medal* (1986); *The Letter of Marque* (1988); *The Thirteen-Gun Salute* (1989); *The Nutmeg of Consolation* (1992); *Clarissa Oakes* (1993). London: Collins.

Rogers, John G. *Origins of Sea Terms*. 2d ed. Mystic, Connecticut: Mystic Seaport Museum, 1985.

Sleightholme, J. D. *A.B.C. for Yachtsmen*. London: Adlard Coles, 1965.

Smollett, Tobias. *The Adventures of Roderick Random*. Oxford, England: Oxford University Press, 1981.

Smyth, W. H. *The Sailor's Word Book*. London: Blackie and Son, 1867.

Warner, Oliver. *The British Navy: A Concise History*. London: Thames and Hudson, 1975.

Whitlock, Peter C. et al. *The Country Life Book of Nautical Terms under Sail*. London: Hamlyn, 1978.

Dictionaries

Brewer, E. C., ed. *Brewer's Dictionary of Phrase and Fable*. London: Cassell,1981.

Delbridge, A., ed. *The Macquarie Dictionary*. St. Leonards, Victoria: Macquarie Library, 1981.

Funk, Wilfred John. *Word Origins and Their Romantic Stories*. Reprint ed. New York: Bell, 1978.

Hunter, Robert. *Universal Dictionary of the English Language*. New York: Collier, 1897.

Little, William; H. W. Fowler; and J. Coulson. The Shorter Oxford English Dictionary on Historical Principles. Oxford, England: Clarendon, 1962.

McAdam, E. L., Jr. and G. Milne. *Dictionary, Samuel Johnson (1755): A Modern Selection*. London, 1982.

Murray, J. H. et al., ed. *Oxford English Dictionary*. Oxford, England, 1970.

Partridge, Eric. *Origins: A Short Etymological Dictionary of Modern English*. New York: Greenwich House, 1983.

Webster's New Twentieth Century Dictionary of the English Language. Unabridged, 2d ed. Cleveland and New York: World Publishing Company, 1965.

Weekley, Ernest. *An Etymological Dictionary of Modern English*. Reprint ed. New York: Dover, 1967.